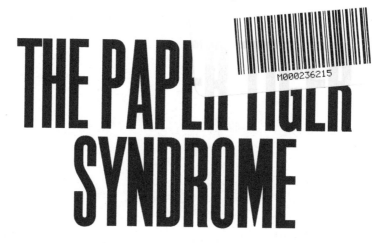

THE PAPER TIGER SYNDROME

How to Liberate Yourself from the Illusion of Fear

Rebecca A. Ward, LMFT, SEP, PCC

Published by Original Blueprint Press
originalblueprintpress.com

Published by Original Blueprint Press
originalblueprintpress.com

Printed in the USA
Cover Design by Justin Metz
Interior illustrations by Lea Androic
Charts by Rebecca Ward, et. al.
Anatomy illustrations by Lauren Hugdahl
Copyright © 2022 by Rebecca Ward

ISBN: 9780578359861

In memory of my sons, Nathaniel and Eliot,
whose brief lives on this planet made me who I am today.

I would like to praise my Infinite Source for the gift of this extraordinary life. Words cannot describe how grateful I am for every moment I am here to experience the unfolding of this remarkable and extraordinary mystery.

I would like to thank my village—every soul who has walked this path with me and taught me what it means to belong.

In no particular order, thank you to all my teachers, healers, and fellow practitioners, including Peter Levine, Kathy Kain, Stephen Terrell, Theresa Lumiere, Gabor Maté, Berns Galloway, Ariel Giaretto, Rob Wergin, Janina Fisher, Christina Lehnherr, Marsha Angus, and Carolyn Cooper. I am eternally grateful to each of you for helping me rediscover my Original Blueprint®.

To all my clients—you are my greatest teachers.

My dear family and friends—I am deeply grateful for all the support you have given me, especially my mother and father who gave me life, my father who taught me what's important, and to my mother who stood by me through it all. I could not have been on this remarkable journey without all of you, dear ones.

Special thanks to my editors, Kuwana Haulsey and Randy Peyser of Author One Stop, Inc., for their extraordinary work in helping me publish this book at a time when the world needs it most. I also want to acknowledge my colleague, Donna Carter, for generously devoting her time and energy to give the book a final review and edit through the lens of trauma—I am deeply grateful.

Lastly to you, the reader. You are the reason why I wrote this book. In your devotion to heal, I hope this book brings you closer to your Original Blueprint®.

paper tiger

[pa per | \ ˈpā-pər · ti ger | \ ˈtī-gər] *noun*

: something—or someone—that appears to be a threat, but in reality, is powerless.

" "

There is no greater illusion than fear.

- Lao Tzu

> **"**
> *The medicine is already within the pain and suffering. You just have to look deeply and quietly. Then you realize it has been there the whole time.*
>
> - Wisdom from the Native American oral tradition

PREFACE

Inside every one of us lies a hidden landscape that is the embodiment of boundless, unconditional love. If you could map this landscape, the map would detail the wide-open savannas and curving shorelines of your original self—the person you were intended to be when you first entered the world. We've all had glimpses of this version of ourselves, just as we've also witnessed it resurface in others. It's in the moments when you see a beautiful sunrise and feel gratitude in your heart. It's in the infectious joy of an infant who can't control her belly laugh. It's in the sudden impulse to do a kind deed for a stranger. These are the moments when we're back in touch with ourselves.

When you have a clear connection to this Self—what I call your Original Blueprint®—you feel open and spacious and fully alive. Fear no longer has the power to control your thoughts and actions because you have an intuitive understanding of your connection to the rest of the world. That connection allows you to be courageous, step out from your inhibitions, and live fearlessly. When misfortune strikes, you have the tools to find your way back to your center and liberate yourself from suffering.

This book is a roadmap to guide you on that journey back home. It's brimming with examples—from numerous clients of mine, as well as my own life—that describe the journey you're about to embark upon, as you clear away old survival strategies and conditioned beliefs and make way for a present, whole, and connected Self.

Before we begin, make sure that you have a personal journal to write down your thoughts and complete the exercises or use *The Paper Tiger Companion Workbook* (sold separately at www. IrisInstitute.com and hereafter referred to as the "Companion

Workbook"). The *Companion Workbook* is a beautiful, full-color interactive and downloadable workbook, formatted specifically to guide you along this journey with all the rituals and exercises in Parts Two and Three. Having said that, any journal will suffice, as long as you use it to faithfully record the thoughts, feelings, and insights that arise as a result of your work.

You'll also need to set aside reflective time to complete the various rituals and exercises. And I strongly encourage you to integrate at least one ritual you learn from this book into your life on a daily basis because even after you've completed the book the work continues. There are also more resources on my website at IrisInstitute.com that you can access to continue to stay in the work, including printable worksheets, videos and guided recordings of the rituals and exercises from Parts Two and Three of this book.

Sometimes the fear, stress, and uncertainty of life—your paper tigers—can feel overwhelming. They are not. To overcome them, you need only acquire the right tools. Having said that, I must acknowledge that this road is far from easy. Many people who begin this kind of healing journey do so because they've experienced trauma. In fact, I first began my journey after a series of intense traumas that culminated in a diagnosis that nearly ended my life early.

It's very common for people who face loss, hardship, and suffering to ask, "*Is this all there is? Is this what my life was meant to be? Will I ever feel myself again? Will I ever be at peace?*" Obviously, no single book can magically repair all your traumas. But the rituals and exercises revealed here will support the healing process in ways that would be inaccessible through traditional methods.

However, I must also offer a word of caution. If you're someone who's endured complex trauma and you're just beginning your healing journey, you may need additional support. In that case, this book may not be the appropriate starting place, unless you also have the assistance of a licensed therapist who is trained in a trauma modality. For those who've already begun a healing journey, working independently should enhance the progress you've already made.

If you're not sure which path is right for you, I suggest taking the Adverse Childhood Experiences (ACEs) survey, included here. The Centers for Disease Control and Prevention (CDC) defines adverse childhood experiences as, "potentially traumatic events that occur in childhood (0-17 years) …ACEs are linked to chronic health problems, mental illness, and substance misuse in adulthood. ACEs can also negatively impact education and job opportunities…"

The stressors of cumulative adversity have far-reaching effects that we're only just beginning to fully understand. According to the ACEs study, there are ten types of childhood trauma. Five are personal — physical abuse, verbal abuse, sexual abuse, physical neglect, and emotional neglect. The others relate to how a child experiences her interactions with different family members: a parent who is an alcoholic, a mother who is a victim of domestic violence, a family member in jail, a family member diagnosed with a mental illness, and the disappearance of a parent through divorce, death, or abandonment.

To take the survey, read the following questions. For each question where you answer "yes," give yourself one point. If you score three or higher, you may be at risk of experiencing long-term consequences from early abuse and/or neglect. Scores of three or higher have been linked to chronic disease in adulthood, social and emotional difficulties, depression, interpersonal violence and even suicide.

But getting a high ACE score is, by no means, a sentence to a life of misery. There's always *plenty* of hope. With the right support, people with very high ACE scores can lead healthy, happy lives and even be a source of inspiration. I believe that the ability to thrive despite past traumas is an indication of your incredible resilience. That is certainly true for me—I was an ACE kid.

The following survey is meant to be a point of reference, rather than a diagnosis. But I hope it will be a helpful place to start for anyone who has questions or concerns in this area.

ACE SURVEY
ADVERSE CHILDHOOD EXPERIENCES

Q: While you were growing up, during your first 18 years of life:

1. **Did a parent or other adult in the household often or very often...**
   Swear at you, insult you, put you down or humiliate you?
   or
   Act in a way that made you afraid that you might be physically hurt?

   ☐ Yes   ☐ No   If yes, enter 1 _____

2. **Did a parent or other adult in the household often or very often...**
   Push, grab, slap, or throw something at you?
   or
   Ever hit you so hard that you had marks or were injured?

   ☐ Yes   ☐ No   If yes, enter 1 _____

3. **Did an adult or person at least 5 years older than you ever...**
   Touch or fondle you or have you touch their body in a sexual way?
   or
   Attempt or actually have oral, anal, or vaginal intercourse with you?

   ☐ Yes   ☐ No   If yes, enter 1 _____

4. **Did you often or very often feel that ...**
   No one in your family loved you or thought you were important or special?
   or
   Your family didn't look out for each other, feel close to each other, or support each other?

   ☐ Yes   ☐ No   If yes, enter 1 _____

5. **Did you often or very often feel that ...**
   You didn't have enough to eat, had to wear dirty clothes, and had no one to protect you?
   or
   Your parents were too drunk or high to take care of you or take you to the doctor if you needed it?

   ☐ Yes   ☐ No   If yes, enter 1 _____

6. **Were your parents ever separated or divorced?**

   ☐ Yes   ☐ No   If yes, enter 1 _____

7. **Was your mother or stepmother:**
   Often or very often pushed, grabbed, slapped, or had something thrown at her?
   or
   Sometimes, often, or very often kicked, bitten, hit with a fist, or hit with something hard?
   or
   Ever repeatedly hit over at least a few minutes or threatened with a gun or knife?

   ☐ Yes   ☐ No   If yes, enter 1 _____

8. Did you live with anyone who was a problem drinker or alcoholic, or who used street drugs?

☐ Yes   ☐ No   If yes, enter 1 _____

9. Was a household member depressed or mentally ill, or did a household member attempt suicide?

☐ Yes   ☐ No   If yes, enter 1 _____

10. Did a household member go to prison?

☐ Yes   ☐ No   If yes, enter 1 _____

As you tally your score, remember that there are many additional factors, which determine how resilient an individual will be in the face of trauma, abuse, or neglect. If you choose to work with a trauma therapist in conjunction with reading this book, it can only improve your personal outcome. There are many skilled trauma practitioners available through several directories, including:

Somatic Experiencing® International (SEI)
www.traumahealing.org

Sensorimotor Psychotherapy
www.sensorimotorpsychotherapy.org

Eye Movement Desensitization and Reprocessing (EMDR)
www.emdr.com

You might also check your local healthcare facilities for trauma support groups.

Whatever path you choose, the methods that you'll learn here can help you to embody life-long positive changes and lead you back to a place of centered calm and joy—no matter what life throws at you. Chronic fear and past experiences will no longer have the power to determine your future. But the lessons that you take from those experiences will shape how you show up in every other facet of life.

Learning to tame your paper tigers and embody your Original Blueprint® will create a space for unconditional love to flow to and through you and out into the world. Then, you'll be able to embrace all of life's lessons and flourish under any circumstance.

❝❝

She could no longer borrow from the future to ease her present grief.

- Nathaniel Hawthorne

It All Starts Here...My Story

The knock at the door caught me off guard. I wasn't expecting anyone and wondered who would show up at my house in the middle of the day unannounced. Whoever it was would have to wait, as I rushed through the tiny apartment, getting ready for class. If I was late again, my professor would kill me. I grabbed my jacket and car keys, while trying unsuccessfully to balance a stack of heavy textbooks and shove them into my worn-out canvas backpack.

The knock came again, this time even louder and more insistent.

"Who is it?" I yelled.

"Columbia Police Department."

I stopped. My heart jumped in my chest. Why would the police be at my door? Was someone sick? Had there been an accident? Different scenarios raced through my mind, each a little bit more frightening than the last. I slid my books onto the kitchen table and slowly walked towards the door. Taking a deep breath, I gripped the doorknob and swung the door open. Two somber looking officers stood in front of me with their hats in their hands.

"Yes," I said. "Can I help you?"

"Rebecca Ward?" one of the officers asked.

"Yes," I replied. "What's going on?"

Instead of answering my question, one of the officers reached out and handed me a card with a phone number on it.

"Call this number."

"Could you tell me what this is about?" I asked again, as my heart continued to race.

The officer didn't reply directly to my question. "Please just call the number," he said. And with that, they left and began walking back down the hallway.

I closed the door and stared at the card in my hand. Then I reached for my phone and immediately dialed the number.

"Denver Coroner's Office," said a voice on the other end of the line.

Oh no.

My voice began to shake as I said, "Hello, I was just given this phone number by two officers from my police department. They said to call you."

"Could you identify yourself, please."

"My name is Rebecca Ward," I said.

There was a slight pause. Then the coroner asked, "Who is Terry Ward to you?"

"He's my father."

He sighed and said, "I'm so sorry to have to tell you like this, but your father is dead."

I froze as the coroner's words began to coarse through my body.

"Okay thank you," I managed to say. Then the phone fell from my hand and my legs gave way. I dropped to the floor, sobbing. My entire body began to tingle as the waves of shock overpowered me.

All I could think was: *He's gone. I'm all alone. It's all up to me now. I have to figure out life by myself.*

My father and I were just starting a new relationship when he died. For most of my twenty years, our relationship had been volatile and strained, to say the least. There had been long stretches of time when he was absent from my life altogether. In his absence, my mother struggled to provide food and shelter for me and my sister. As the child of an alcoholic, I'd grown accustomed to his absence; callouses had grown over the tender spots in my heart where I'd longed for his presence.

But then, about two years before he passed, we reconnected. And for the first time, things were going really well between us. He was kind and interested and present in my life, albeit from a distance once I left to go to college. He'd finally become the best version of himself, at least where I was concerned. It's what I'd always wanted—a close bond with my dad.

And then, just when we were getting to know each other, he was gone.

When I lost my father, anything that ever felt like security and stability was gone. Despite all my experiences to the contrary, I still clung to the notion that fathers are meant to be a child's protector. With him gone, the feeling of fear that washed over me was unlike anything I'd ever experienced. It changed me in ways that I would only come to fully understand years later.

I was alone in a small Midwest college town, with the rest of my family over a thousand miles away. There would be no one there to support me, no one to come and help me up if I should stumble and fall.

From that day forward, the desire for security became the driving force in my life. I became afraid to take chances, afraid of the unexpected twists and turns that life inevitably brings. I was afraid to be me. The choices that I started making—in everything from choosing a career to finding a partner—were motivated by my overwhelming need for security and stability. I needed to prove that I could make it on my own. And that meant making some hard choices.

I wanted to study photojournalism and travel the world to shed light on the injustices. But after my father died, I ignored that desire and immersed myself in a course of study that would lead directly to higher paying, stable jobs. I took the business route, even though I had no strong interest in the field. But in my mind, working a corporate job for a well-established company translated into steady paychecks and real security.

The fear of the unknown had hovered over me like a dark cloud since I was a little girl in the years when my home often felt like a war zone. Losing my father just made it even more ingrained in me. When you have an addicted parent, you learn to expect chaos and instability; you very quickly discover that their primary relationship is with alcohol, or whatever their drug of choice might be. You figure out how to accommodate them in order to survive.

I became an expert at using survival strategies and coping mechanisms to get through. I transformed into the quiet child in the household who didn't rock the boat. I kept my feelings inside and learned not to express myself. It was easier to isolate, drifting off into my own world for long periods of time. At least then I felt like I could be in control—safe from the constant upheaval in my family. The message I internalized was: *"If I'm silent and don't ask for too much, I'll be safe."*

In addition to my father's alcoholism, my parents divorced in the late 70s, when I was seven years old. Back then, divorced women didn't have many options for financial independence. They couldn't do basic things like get a credit card or a home loan. My mother was no exception. Financial stability seemed impossible, as she struggled to pay the bills with no support, while raising two daughters. Through no fault of her own, she didn't have the time or the energy to devote to me or my older sister. She was just trying to survive, day by day.

Those early experiences taught me that life was precarious, prone to turmoil and dysfunction. I began to believe that men were not to be relied on to provide for their families when times got hard. I believed that women needed to be completely self-sufficient and fiercely independent to survive.

Thus, my father's passing also brought me face-to-face with a painful paradox: I didn't know how to reconcile the social conditioning that "fathers are protectors" with the reality of feeling unsafe around him. Because my father was unpredictable when I was a child, I lived with a primal fear of not having my basic needs met. My fear shaped how I saw myself (small, isolated, unworthy) and the world around me (harsh, cruel, volatile).

By the time I found myself sobbing on the living room floor mourning the loss of my father, I had already long ago lost myself. My grief, mixed with my fear of what could go even more horribly wrong in the future, was so overwhelming that my body shut down, causing a rift between my physical and emotional self that would take decades to repair.

From that day forward, I doggedly pursued a life that didn't fulfill me. I chased after money, accomplishment, and accolades as a substitute for the validation that I so desperately wanted from my father. But nothing external would ever be able to provide what I really needed: the understanding that I was enough.

No matter how "successful" I became, the fear that I wouldn't be able to take care of myself haunted me at every turn. Deep inside, I felt like a failure. No matter how beautiful my home, how much education and credentialing I amassed or how much money I had in the bank, I continued to ask myself, *How am I going to live? What am I going to do? How am I going to take care of myself?* The relentless vigilance left me feeling isolated. It was so difficult for me to ask for support from anyone, even people that I knew loved me. My life was all about getting the right job, and then angling for a better job with a bigger paycheck. Like many other people, I never stopped to ask myself, *To what end? When will it ever be enough? When will I ever be enough?*

As the years passed, my fears pulled me further away from the path I'd always dreamed of when I was young. Rather than becoming a globe trotting photojournalist, I climbed the corporate ladder. I had credibility, seniority, money, job security and the respect of my peers—and I was miserable. My health declined and my relationships withered. Life felt meaningless.

The idea that I could thrive never occurred to me. Simply being content with myself—not constantly worried about the next big "what if"—was unimaginable. I just went through the motions: head off to work in the morning, come back home at night to crawl into bed and get up and do the same thing all over again. In retrospect, I now know that I had no connection at all to my body. And I don't mean how my body looked on the outside, but more about what it felt like to be in my body. I was a complete stranger to myself.

In my romantic relationships, I repeated familiar patterns that re-created the chaos that I'd so despised in my childhood. I unconsciously chose partners who were volatile and unreliable, who never made me the priority. Many were drug users, philanderers, emotionally abusive, unavailable, detached, or toxic in some other way. Deep in my heart I wished for a partnership based in love, honesty, and mutual respect. I just didn't believe I deserved it and I didn't know how to recognize it.

In my early thirties, I met a man who I hoped would be the partner I always wanted. We married about eighteen months after we met. Looking back, I am able to clearly see the red flags in our relationship. But, at the time, I was so hopeful that *this time* things would be different; I wanted my marriage to be the one soft place that I could land when the stressors of life became too much to handle on my own. (Out of respect for his privacy, you will discover throughout this chapter that my former husband's name and some details of the events have been omitted.)

About two years into the marriage, we decided to have a baby. At first, things went better than we could have hoped. I quickly became pregnant with twin boys and for the first several months the pregnancy appeared to be healthy and uneventful. But on August 7, 2007, everything changed.

It was the beginning of my third trimester. I'd begun to have serious doubts about my marriage. All the old, dysfunctional patterns that I'd seen in my other relationships had resurfaced with a vengeance. We argued often and I began to lose trust in him. One Friday afternoon, I was having what I thought was a harmless conversation with my husband when he snapped and verbally laid into me so viciously that his words took my breath away. I froze in fear, wondering if the situation had suddenly escalated beyond my control.

In a split second of clarity, I knew that our marriage wouldn't survive. The writing had been on the wall and I couldn't ignore it anymore. Things would only get worse over time and, at some point in the near future, the situation would be so unstable that it would fall apart entirely. When that happened, I wondered, what would become of me and the babies? I rushed to defuse the conflict by using my old survival strategy—stay silent. It worked. The only thing I cared about was keeping my unborn children safe. *Oh no, I've made a mistake, I thought. I can't raise children like this. This isn't a place where children can grow up feeling secure and happy. What am I going to do?*

My husband stormed off and left me alone in our home. I was shaking and terrified, but grateful to be unharmed. When he came home again, he acted as if nothing had happened. But I couldn't forget. Over and over, I kept thinking, *I can't bring children into this situation. This isn't safe. We aren't safe.* On the surface, things seemed to be pretty normal. Yet, I knew that it would never be normal again.

That evening, I started feeling cramps in my abdomen and back that worsened as the evening progressed. At the time, having never experienced it before, I didn't recognize that the pains were labor contractions. While I may have been in my third trimester, it was still far too early in the pregnancy for me to be going into labor. So, instead of tuning into my body and seeking help when I so clearly needed it, I remained shut down.

For the next forty-eight hours, I sank into deep denial. I drifted into a disembodied state where my body shut down, rendering me numb from feeling anything that could cause me further pain. I was disconnected, listless, and dead inside. My body froze in an attempt to keep me safe.

I had a doctor's appointment first thing Monday morning and I'd decided to tell my obstetrician about my symptoms when I arrived for my appointment. But I woke up that morning to find that I was bleeding. Trying to control my panic, I drove myself to the hospital. After a thorough examination, the doctor confirmed that I'd been having contractions. She said that I'd need to stay in the hospital where they'd put me on a machine that would attempt to slow down my contractions to stop the labor.

Stopping labor was critical because the babies were still far too small to survive outside the womb. If I gave birth, their chances for survival were slim. Even under the best circumstances, being so premature would likely result in severe, lifelong defects. The doctors monitored me continuously to see if any of their interventions were working. But the contractions wouldn't stop. In fact, they got more intense and began to come closer and closer together.

Later that evening my doctor walked into my room and said, "You know, we're going to continue to try to save your babies. We're holding out hope."

And I remember thinking to myself, *Well, I don't know what she means by that. But I'm sure she'll figure this out.*

The next morning, however, the doctor came in and sat down to share devastating news.

"You're going to be delivering the babies," she told me. "You need to prepare for this." Again, I didn't know what that meant. I was still stuck in a fog of denial. My mind decided to interpret her words literally: *I'm just preparing to give birth.*

A nurse wheeled me into a cold, gray delivery room where my husband was waiting. That's when one of the doctors finally looked at me and said, "We don't think they're going to make it. We'll try and see if we can get the second one to stay in the womb, but it may not be possible. The babies will be alive when you deliver them. But they will probably only live for a few hours. And then they will be gone."

I didn't question the medical team. I didn't cry. I just laid there, frozen, unable to think for myself or process the devastating news. I barely felt the long, thin catheter pierce my lower back as they administered the epidural. During the procedure, I remember a nurse asking me, "Ok, so when they come, do you want to see them? What do you want to do?"

I didn't even know how to answer the question.

"Um," I stammered, "what, what do people usually do in these cases?"

"This doesn't happen that often," she said, "but when it happens, people usually want to see the baby."

"Oh," I said, "well, then that's what I should do."

The doctors and nurses stifled their own sobs as the labor proceeded. Periodically, I would hear the nurses whispering to each other, saying things like, "This has never happened before. I've never seen this happen before." Their words penetrated my heart as I began to think, *Why me? What have I done?*

A short while later, I delivered my first baby—a perfect, tiny little boy. When they put him in my arms, the dam that had been holding back all my sorrow and grief broke open. A howling sound came out of me that I had never made before. It was grief erupting from the depths of my soul.

As I cried out, I heard a voice, which I believe was the voice of my God, saying to me, *there will be time for grief later. Right now, enjoy every moment you have with them. Grieve later.*

When I heard that voice of wisdom, I stopped crying. I stopped howling and looked down at my son. I studied every inch of his little body—studied his little fingers and his little feet with their perfect tiny toes, and his beautiful little legs and his peaceful face. His eyes hadn't opened yet. He wasn't far enough along for that to have happened, but the rest of him was fully formed and wonderful.

We named him Nathaniel, after the novelist, Nathaniel Hawthorne. I still remember every inch of Nathaniel, to this day. I remember holding him. I remember feeling an indescribable love for him, a love that still brings me to tears and makes my heart ache. He was the most beautiful thing I'd ever seen. Absolutely breathtaking. As I was holding him, the doctor said, "We're not going to be able to save the second one. So, you've got to prepare. The second baby is coming."

About thirty minutes later, I delivered Eliot, named after the poet T.S. Eliot. He was just as perfect and as beautiful as his brother. Eliot had a little birthmark on his shoulder. The nurses swaddled the boys and handed them both back to me. I held them in my arms with my husband at my side, Nathaniel on my left and Eliot on my right. They were alive and breathing gently on their own. But unable to survive.

Time stopped. I spent those fleeting moments fully present, relishing their magnificent lives. About four hours later, Nathaniel and Eliot passed away within minutes of each other.

That day was the most extraordinary day of my life. To experience life beginning and life ending as book ends on the same day changed me in every possible way; I'd touched the thin veil between this world and the next in ways that most people never have the chance to experience. I knew that I would never be the same.

The joy I felt that day was unlike anything that I'd ever known. I was blessed with the opportunity to welcome these two souls into the world. And while they were here only momentarily, they brought so much grace and joy into my life. Those few hours with my sons taught me the most incredible lesson that I was only at the beginning of understanding at the time—to feast on every moment of life. It was humbling and amazing and life-changing.

But trying to adjust to my new reality in the weeks and months that followed was unbearable. Grief pulsated throughout my body like a second heartbeat. I thought the pain would lessen over time, but it didn't. It just got tucked down and buried deep inside me, wrapped in a cloak of shame.

In his book, *When the Body Says No: Exploring the Stress-Disease Connection,* Dr. Gabor Maté speaks about the avoidance of shame when he said: *"Shame is the deepest of the 'negative emotions,' a feeling we will do almost anything to avoid. Unfortunately, our abiding fear of shame impairs our ability to see reality."*

I avoided shame and carried its heavy weight in my heart for the next ten years. I regularly agonized over the notion that I couldn't save my children, that my body had betrayed me. Hidden beneath the shame was an even more insidious belief that it was my fault that they didn't survive. As every mother does, I felt a primal responsibility to protect my babies. It may have been irrational, but I felt like I was responsible for their deaths. And since "I had killed them," I believed I deserved whatever punishment life had in store for me.

These toxic thoughts, feelings and fears haunted me, even though I did everything I could think of to move on and make healthy changes in my life. I left my husband, thankful that at least I'd never have to endure that volatility and destructiveness again.

I changed jobs and progressed in my career. Most importantly, I began a life-saving practice of daily prayer and meditation. But for years, I couldn't shake my grief, shame, and fear; I transformed into a shadow of the person that I was meant to be.

Five years after the loss of my boys, I received more devastating news.

For months I'd been experiencing a range of troubling symptoms, but I couldn't pinpoint anything specific. I'd always been a healthy person, so I was concerned enough to make an appointment with my doctor. They ran a full battery of tests and sent me home. For days, I tried to distract myself as I waited for my test results. When I felt fear stirring in my chest, pulling me off balance, I meditated to quiet my mind and return to my center. But the waiting was tough. I was terrified.

In what I can only call an incredible cosmic coincidence, I received three separate calls on the same day with lab results that confirmed three separate primary cancers. Two of the cancers were potentially lethal. Each call felt like another blow to my heart.

To say that I was overwhelmed would be an understatement; I had no idea what to do. *How can this be happening?*, I wondered. *How much is one person supposed to take? Is this punishment for not saving my babies?* My first instinct was to retreat into myself, to surrender to fear—fear of the unknown, fear of dying, fear that I might never get a chance to live the life that I had always wanted to live. Fear stalked me, from the moment I opened my eyes in the morning until I closed them at night. In my heart, I yearned to be brave and resilient. But I could feel my body shutting down…the hollowness in my chest, the weakness in my legs, the fogginess in my brain that tried to shield me from concentrating on my immense fear. I felt **sheer terror.**

But I refused to give up. The will to survive kept me going and searching for answers. I visited numerous specialists, choosing surgeons, and mapping out a treatment plan. When I found myself completely immobilized with fear, my support system saved me. My desperation for anything that felt safe was so strong that I had no other choice but to accept help. In these early days, that desperation became a gift. For the first time, I was learning how to receive support and the people around me stepped up in ways that I never could've imagined before. My family and close friends surrounded me with all the love and support I needed. Prayer circles began to form in networks across the world.

Before each surgery, the medical team would stand together to pray for me. My mother—a nurse herself—was a constant support; the experience strengthened our relationship. Most of all, I had an unflappable faith in my Infinite Source. I prayed, I meditated, and I envisioned myself in a body that was resilient, healthy, and full of aliveness.

Over time, I got stronger, more resilient, and more confident. I stopped *hoping* and started *believing*. I trusted that I would be okay no matter what.

The doctors' diagnoses made me realize that I'd suppressed fear and shame so deep inside that these emotions literally manifested as *dis*-ease in my body. I produced cancers in the parts of my body where I'd held unresolved grief for years. One of the cancers that I developed was the same cancer that had taken my father's life decades earlier. Two other cancers grew in my body where reproduction occurs—where I last held my boys. The only way my body could alleviate the grief is to excise it from my body.

My body had been holding the full weight of a grief so intense, that I couldn't allow myself to face it for fear that it would destroy me. Touching it would have been like touching molten lava at the core of a volcano. I was terrified that I would disintegrate and turn to ash. Just because I hadn't been able to face the pain, however, didn't mean that it wasn't still affecting me. That volcano inside me had imploded and the searing lava flowed deep, deep into my core. That searing lava became cancer because there was no other place for it to go.

For the next seven years, I fought my way through multiple surgeries and treatments, redoubling my commitment to healing. And this time nothing was off limits. The healing journey back to my authentic self was a winding, bumpy road. I took detours, got lost and sometimes went backwards. There were times of great fear, uncertainty, and indecision. But there were also moments of incredible clarity, expansion, and courage.

I left my business career, went back to school, and trained to be a therapist. I explored every healing modality that I came across to see which were effective and produced tangible results. I studied under all kinds of healers from both Eastern and Western philosophies: energy healers, therapists, body workers—you name it. I immersed myself completely in the science and the spirituality of healing.

Though I tried many different approaches to heal myself of cancer, I never ignored or neglected the traditional treatments from my doctors. I also learned how important it is to self-advocate and trust my own wisdom when it comes to personal wellbeing. I sought to enhance treatments by doing my own work on healing my body. There were many points of intersection where the work of traditional doctors and therapists could potentially be enhanced by my own healing work, along with a wide array of non-traditional modalities that offered promising results.

Eventually, my search led me to discover my new career—the field of *somatic therapy*. Through my own somatic therapy, I learned the secret to re-connecting my mind and body; the techniques practiced in this discipline taught me how to release fear, heal unresolved trauma and create a direct access point to the authentic self, which I'd begun to call my Original Blueprint®. I also learned the power of suggestion—how our words can shape how our bodies respond to the world around us and inside of us.

I fully embraced this new ability to heal the fears and the

traumas of my past, while embodying abundant physical and emotional health. I felt a renewed will to live and an abiding faith in something that was going to carry me through every hardship. Yes, there were times when the old fears arose. I am human. But I'd learned to stay primarily within my window of resilience, where I could witness my emotions without succumbing to them or losing my sense of equilibrium.

Working with my body, specifically my nervous system, showed me how to heal the core wounds that had manifested in my body as lethal disease. I finally faced the fact that I'd been fearfully holding onto a lifetime of unspoken grief and disappointment, which had culminated with the devastating loss of my boys and then cancer.

Working with my own therapist allowed me to delve deep into my unconscious, back to the days leading up to the loss of my boys. I was able to go back and re-live the moments leading up to their birth to uncover what led to the loss. In one session, I became aware of a powerful and unconscious exchange I had with them that Friday evening before they passed. Energetically, without being conscious of it, I sent them this message: *I can see clearly that the situation we're in may not be the life you want to live and if that's how you feel, I want you to know that it's okay if you choose not to stay. I love you both so much that I will give my body permission to release you from this life and hold the grief of losing you so that you don't suffer. I will let you go. That's how much I love you.*

Bringing that dialogue into my conscious mind released me from the shame and grief I'd been holding. I realized that I hadn't failed to protect them. I had loved them unconditionally—a mother's love that allowed me the strength to let them go. Understanding the emotional subtext of loss liberated me. I could feel God's love for me and my boys.

Understanding those unconscious moments with Nathaniel

and Eliot allowed me to see from a much deeper vantage point. Underneath loss, no matter how great, is a sea of unconditional love. It's the love that we feel when we're connected to the infinite Universe, when we realize that there's no separation, that the universe exists in us and around us.

This divine love is in every human being, every creature in the world. As human beings, we're micro-manifestations of the infinite universe that binds us together and makes us part of every other living thing. There's no "me versus you" or "us versus them" or "black versus white." When we see that we're connected to the infinite universe, everyone matters. When you hurt, I hurt. When I hurt, you hurt. We learn compassion, kindness, and respect—to truly bear witness to each other's suffering as if we are one—because we *are* One.

If we hold onto an abiding faith in the love that connects us all to our Source, we're able to transcend the fear and the survival strategies that keep us small. We understand that we're meant to feel safe and spacious, loving and kind; this is our natural state of being. We're meant to revel in our connection to every being in this world, whether seen or unseen. And we're all here to learn how to let go of our fears and to support others in doing the same.

What I discovered, and what I've been teaching people ever since, is that our fears aren't in our hearts or our minds, as most people believe. *Fear resides in our bodies.* Just as our bodies create the conditions for us to feel fear, they also create the conditions for us to feel safe—regardless of what may be going on in the world. If you believe what I believe—that every experience we have in life happens by design—it becomes easier to recognize that there are no mistakes. Mistakes are ways that the soul grows. Embrace them as opportunities for deeper learning. Each time we overcome something, we inch closer and closer to our Original Blueprint®.

Our work on earth is to reconnect with our Original Blueprint®—it's the knowing we have inside us that tells us there's something else, something more, to who we *really* are. We go through the hardships of life, staying small, being afraid to take a risk or afraid to embrace change; fear convinces us that to step off our roller coaster is dangerous. So, we drag ourselves through life, waiting for the other shoe to drop. We want the best for ourselves, but we expect the worst. As I discovered in my own life, trying to avoid pain and hardship by staying small is a fool's errand. Facing and releasing fear allows us to liberate ourselves so that we can fully live and appreciate what life offers.

Today, I live a life where I can readily see the beauty in everything. Taking out the trash is joyful for me. As a trauma therapist, I see the potential for renewal and growth in others—a return to joy and the belief that everyone deserves to experience boundless love. When my clients confide their stories of suffering, I hold profound compassion and empathy; I also believe that the best is yet to come. Just like the tides rolling onto shores, each wave brings something new and a clearing of what was. Hang on. It gets better.

Reading this book will be an incredible journey of release and renewal. Trust that if you do the work, if you commit to facing your fears with courage, you will heal and grow with the support of this book. You will return to your original self. Reconnecting the body and spirit back to the mind is the most direct path to that place of power. Yes, you'll have to walk through your fears and suffering. There are no short cuts. But remember—part of why you're here is to feel all your emotions, including your suffering, grief, anger, and shame. The emotions that you resist the most are the ones that lie between where you are now and your beautiful, exquisite self—your Original Blueprint®.

People often think that becoming better and more successful means adding to who you already are—more things, more money, more accomplishments. But the opposite is true. Becoming fully embodied and being at peace *within yourself* is about stripping away everything that you've learned about surviving life. It's about letting go of the illusion of fear, which tricks the mind and body into being terrified of things that aren't real. When you release the illusion, eventually all that's left is your truest nature.

That's where I am now.

Let me be the first to say that I'm not perfect. I don't walk around in a state of bliss every moment of the day. But I do have the tools to quickly get myself back to center when life knocks me off balance. I know how to live courageously and to be of service to others, while creating a life that I truly and fearlessly appreciate.

That's what this book is going to help you do, too.

SET YOUR INTENTION

Before we begin this journey together, take a moment to write down what you hope to walk away with when you complete this book.

My intention with this book is to walk away with

(more peace, contentment, etc. and/or less stress, anxiety, etc.)

_____

_____

_____

_____

_____

At the end of this journey, return here to see what's different.

PART
ONE

WHAT'S *REALLY* DRIVING US

> **"**
>
> *In response to threat and injury, animals, including humans, execute biologically based, non-conscious action patterns that prepare them to meet the threat and defend themselves.*
>
> - Peter A. Levine

INTRODUCTION
Understanding Human Wiring

In Part One, you will learn the fundamentals of how fear runs aspects of the human experience—its origins and how it affects daily life. The understanding of your human wiring will help you build a stronger awareness of how your body and mind are wired to survive, to keep you safe, and to help you flourish and thrive. At the end of Part One, you will have the essential knowledge you need to step confidently into the exercises and rituals found in Parts Two and Three, all of which are designed to bring you closer to your Original Blueprint®.

As a reminder, Parts Two and Three are designed to bring you into the exercises and rituals; when you begin Part Two, you will need to download the *Companion Workbook* at IrisInstitute. com or have a personal journal on hand.

I hope you find that expanding your somatic intelligence is a rewarding experience for you. Enjoy!

> *I wish I could show you, when you are lonely or in darkness,*
> *the astonishing light of your own being.*
>
> - Hafiz

CHAPTER ONE

Taming Your Inner Tiger

Can you remember a time when you felt completely fearless, blissful, and alive? Do you recall when you had faith that every moment of your life was sacred, even the ones that caused the greatest suffering, when you knew, without a doubt, that the world was safe and that you were loved unconditionally? That sense of peace, that divine connection, is your natural state of being. It's the truth of who you are and your birthright. Yet, very few of us experience this kind of harmony as part of our everyday, normal life.

Instead, many of us exist in a state of flux, caught between an innate desire for love and connection, and the fear of the unknown. Fear—masked as everyday stress, fatigue, anxiety, overwhelm and trauma—seems to lurk around every corner. It stalks, like a wild tiger prowling the grasslands, looking for vulnerabilities and weaknesses to exploit. More often than people realize, fear influences key decisions that can have a far-reaching impact on their lives, their families, their communities, and the world.

This tug-of-war between possibility and pain plays out in the minds of every person on this planet, to greater or lesser degree. The desire to transcend that emotional roller coaster keeps people yearning and searching for ways to attune to their authentic selves.

Being connected to your authentic nature allows you to move through life with fluidity and creativity. A spacious heart, an open mind and a safe, well-regulated body become the rule, rather than an elusive exception. As your inner critic fades into the background, courage, contentment, and an expansive outlook on life replace self-judgment. Even the physical pains that have ailed you may begin to fade.

This version of yourself, which I call your *Original Blueprint*®, is the purest form of the human expression of your soul. Tapping into its power is the key to living fiercely, without shame or regret.

Spiritually speaking, we each have a self that we were meant to inhabit in this lifetime. Yet, as soon as we take a body, we become influenced and re-shaped by our experiences. Even in utero, babies respond to events that are happening to their mothers. It's simply part of how humans develop and evolve. It's also part of our human experience that the earliest events in our development tend to be imprinted upon us most deeply. The fears, losses and traumas that happen in life can disrupt our sense of safety and belonging.

But through the eyes of your Original Blueprint®, you have the capacity to see that you are part of the same living, breathing organism as everyone else. If you believe, as I do, that there is no separation between us, you're able to experience real freedom because fear no longer drives everything you believe, think, and do. Instead, love drives you.

Most people would love to live this way. The problem is that few of us know how to get there. That primal tension between fear and love keeps people searching outside of themselves for answers. It tends to shock people when they discover that the path to a fearless and fulfilling life has been with them all along.

It is literally right inside of you.

The most direct way to overcome fear and trauma in your life is to regulate your *physical body*, which then allows you to access the heightened mental, emotional, and spiritual state of your Original Blueprint®.

How is this possible? you may be wondering. *What's the gateway?*

Simply put, the body—specifically the nervous system—is the means by which human beings process sensation. This includes both physical and emotional sensations. When the nervous system is in alignment, we experience physical health and well-being, along with emotional peace and connection. When it's out of alignment and in fear, we experience physical dysregulation, pain, and disease along with emotional upheaval or, in some cases, complete disconnection from our emotions.

The nervous system plays such an outsized role in dictating our perceptions of life because, for most of human history, people had to survive in the wilderness along with all the other animals. The ability to respond quickly to sudden changes often meant the difference between life and death. When our ancestors saw or heard a sign of danger—a movement in the grass, a strange shadow—stress reactions signaled the warning inside their bodies. Consequently, our ancestors developed survival traits that enabled them to escape extinction just long enough to reproduce and pass their genes along to another generation.

The fight-or-flight responses that their nervous systems initiated sped up the heart, increased blood flow to muscles and caused hyperventilation (to get more oxygen for quick reaction). This mobilization in their physiology primed them to respond quickly to a potential predator by searching for it, hiding, or running away. The truly brave might throw a stick and then run away. To this day, these natural threat responses (fight, flight, and freeze) are still our first default responses to any perceived danger in our environment. But once the agricultural era began to take shape, we didn't require nearly as much of our survival instincts.

Fast forward a few hundred thousand years. In today's modern world, "threats" are much more likely to be normal, day-to-day challenges like conversations with the boss, deadlines at work, being stuck in traffic or having a hard conversation with a spouse. But to a human body that's hardwired to search for threat, these normal occurrences can begin to feel like insurmountable, anxiety-producing dangers. It generally goes unnoticed that, most of the time, the perceived threat is a false alarm—a paper tiger.

The term "paper tiger" is shorthand for the myth that the world is a landmine, a danger zone, and the majority of its inhabitants are a threat to society. When a person suffers from Paper Tiger Syndrome, his or her nervous system and primitive brain are constantly misfiring. Their body responds to day-to-day stressors in the same way that it would respond to a genuine, serious threat to their survival.

The only time that your nervous system should mobilize a threat response is when there's actual danger present. Then you're not going to have a choice. Your autonomic nervous system is going to jump in and take over. It will make split second calls in an effort to keep you safe: *Should I run? Should I freeze or should I fight back?*

But when the paper tiger gives you a false read on reality, the brain makes critical decisions based on fear and sensations in your body, which lead the brain to advice such as, *What you're doing isn't safe! Take the safe bet.* Or, *Don't say anything. Keep this quiet. Don't rock the boat.* You can end up designing a whole life that isn't aligned with your authentic nature for the sake of staying safe from something that isn't a real threat. People make choices about who to vote for, who to marry, where to live or what to do for a living from a place of unconscious fear. The consequences can be significant.

But it's very possible to work with the nervous system to regulate it so that the mind and the body are in harmony. You can get to a place where your new way of being is one of peace and contentment, where you know that the world is safe and you feel fully present in your life, and that constant undercurrent of fear no longer has the power to control you. And, you have the tools you need to manage daily stressors—they become easier to handle. The tiger can't stalk you, once you've tamed him and made him your friend.

That is the journey back to your Original Blueprint®.

You must learn to restore the body to a regulated state, if you want to free yourself from years of destructive conditioning fueled by fear. The methods for returning to the Original Blueprint® that we'll learn in this book will provide a clear, step-by-step process for regulating your nervous system; you'll learn how to move away from the over-reactive survival mechanisms that lead to Paper Tiger Syndrome, and toward the freedom of your truest nature.

Imagine the body as a container for your lessons. When an assignment comes up (trauma, unexpected experiences, or challenging events, etc.), your soul is being put to the test. You may not get to choose the tests that come your way, but you do get to choose how you respond to them. You get to decide whether to rely on a nervous system that's dysregulated and constantly misfiring, or a nervous system that's fully regulated and more in control of its responses.

"Your Original Blueprint® is the purest form of the human expression of your soul."

So, how do you want to move through the tough times? How do you heal? How do you break free from old conditioning to live, love and lead through a more expansive lens? How do you release the fears that keep you feeling small and helpless? Which path will you choose to follow?

Have you ever thought to yourself: *This is not the way my life was supposed to be. How did I get here? I don't even recognize myself anymore. I've lost myself.* I don't know very many people who haven't felt that way at one time or another. But you can regain what you've lost. It will take some commitment and a shift in your perspective.

The first step in learning to regulate your nervous system and tame your paper tiger is to stop trying so hard to avoid the experiences that you fear will bring pain or suffering. Instead of resisting and fearing the future, I invite you to accept all the "gifts" that life has to offer and the wisdom that comes with those experiences. Your willingness to grow and embrace life as it comes will open the gateway that will lead you back to your Original Blueprint®.

You can do this!

The Gifts of Suffering

When hardship invades your life, the experience can leave you feeling lost and alone. But suffering doesn't cause the disconnect; it's the attempt to *avoid* suffering that creates the illusion of separation and hardship. In other words, because we human beings fear suffering, we seek to escape it at all costs. When that proves impossible, we desperately try to manage our suffering. Of course, that doesn't work either and results in a cycle of suffering—toxic relationships, poor health, addiction, unfulfilling careers and all the other pitfalls that we face in modern life.

Suffering begins when we assign judgment to our experiences. For example, I held tremendous judgments about the loss of my father, the loss of my children and my cancer diagnoses. I firmly categorized those experiences as negative and terrifying, as many people might in those situations. But as I began to inhabit my own Original Blueprint®, I realized that there were precious gifts inside the suffering that were there to help me grow and learn.

If we don't assign judgment, if we remain neutral, curious, and open, we begin to see that all experiences and all people are here to teach us something. The wonder and mystery of our human expression knows no bounds. We can learn to appreciate everything life has to offer, not just the things that we assign with a "good" label.

Moments of suffering tend to be when you grow the most. People die. Jobs end. Friendships sour. Couples divorce. Everyone faces crises at some point over the course of a lifetime. But if you're able to focus on the lessons, you can set the stage for real growth. Each moment of adversity provides an opportunity for you to get closer to the unconditional love and wisdom of your Original Blueprint®.

Today, I feel more joyful and alive for having come out the other side of my own suffering. I don't wish to change anything about my life experiences. I no longer live in fear of my mortality. I'm here in the moment, present, fully alive, and grateful. I delight in every breath that comes into my body. Each one is a surprise. Each one is a chance to live another precious moment on earth.

The only breath, the only moment that matters, is the one we're in right now. So, the closer we can get to *now*, the closer we are to *being* our Original Blueprint®.

The Body is the Gateway to the Original Blueprint®

Your Original Blueprint® is the part of you that knows abundance is your natural state. It's the inner voice, which says, *I am full. I am satiated. I am content. I am peaceful. I don't need anything or anyone else to feel complete. There's a richness inside of me that's not about what I have. It's about an embodiment of who I am. I'm not trapped by deficit thinking. I don't look at what isn't. I look at what is. I choose to be grateful for what I have, rather than dwelling on what I think I'm missing. I am in full acceptance and appreciation of whatever comes my way, and I will meet these moments with deep gratitude.*

This is more than a change in mindset. It's about developing a body that feels fully alive and present and inhabiting it. If you're really *in* your body, you're less likely to allow yourself to become depleted or sick. You're more likely to welcome things that support your physical, emotional, and spiritual well-being. This method of self-development enables you to personify the sacred plan that you created for your soul before you incarnated on this planet. **And the nervous system is the mechanism that can get you there—it is both what presents paper tigers and what liberates you from them.**

As we've learned, the nervous system drives your automatic reactions to fear. It's also the same mechanism that, when properly regulated, puts you back in touch with your Original Blueprint®. Imagine one path that diverges into two separate roads. The branch of the road that bends toward fear can only lead to further suffering. But the other branch, which bends toward mindfulness and self-regulation, leads you to the gateway of your Original Blueprint®. The idea of a physical path to spiritual liberation is wonderful because it demystifies the process, rather than presenting it as something elusive or nebulous. Of course, the brain has a critical part to play, but in this journey, you'll begin with the body.

Most people aren't conscious of the crucial role that their nervous system plays in their day-to-day functioning. I didn't become aware of it until I began studying the field of somatics (soma is the Greek word for "body"). Essentially, somatic therapy takes the view that the mind, emotions, and sensations within the body are interconnected. When we rely heavily on our mind to the exclusion of our physical intelligence we are locked out of the gateway. That split is then reinforced by the traumas of life, which cause us to feel unsafe in our bodies. But healing that fracture supports the embodiment of our authentic, integrated self.

The autonomic nervous system is designed to instantly sense any threats to our physical safety. Fortunately, our nervous system remains as efficient as it was in primitive times, when it sensed real unequivocal danger lurking in the tall grasses. Today, if someone is coming at you with a gun or there's an avalanche or a devastating earthquake, your body will respond the same way it would have to an attacking saber-toothed tiger. And you want your body to do that. If your body lost the ability to react quickly to legitimate threats, you wouldn't last long in this world.

"The nervous system is the mechanism that reunites you with your Original Blueprint®—it is both what presents paper tigers and what liberates you from them."

But most of the time, the modern world doesn't present the types of threats that we were hardwired to guard against from our primitive days. Saber-toothed tigers don't stalk us anymore. Today, we lead lives that offer us ample protection from the *natural* world.

Of course, real physical threats still can happen at any time and it's an ugly truth that different categories of people can face different levels of safety in our world. Acknowledging this is a fundamental first step because, as the author James Baldwin said, *"Not everything that is faced can be changed, but nothing can be changed until it is faced."* Bias based on race, class, gender, and a host of other labels can profoundly affect how safe we feel and *are* in the world. Black men in the United States, for example, are two to three times more likely to die in police interactions or be imprisoned than their White male counterparts. Black and Indigenous women are two to three times more likely to die from pregnancy-related causes overlooked by their doctors. Outside the US in war-torn parts of the world like Afghanistan, Yemen, and Syria, your chances of survival drop 30%, on average, due to the catastrophic impact of weapons and war. In the US and abroad, people have very different understandings of what it means to feel secure and protected in their environment.

The rest of us who live with the privilege of going about our days in *relative* safety still face stressful deadlines, pressure to achieve, challenges with spouses or children, financial concerns and more. While these things can be stressful, none of them should be setting off survival-level alarm bells in the nervous system.

Yet, they do. And depending on your environment, upbringing and coping skills, your nervous system may be misfiring a lot more often than you think.

These misfires can create exaggerated, prolonged, and even chronic, stress reactions in the body. Chronic stress happens daily. Even the technology we rely on, which supposedly exists to make our lives easier, can undermine us by intensifying feelings of anxiety, depression, and loneliness more than ever before. Nearly two-thirds of all Americans, for example, are suffering from an underlying health condition often brought on by stress, poor diet, or lack of access to good healthcare. In many other countries, these numbers are also rising.

All of these issues legitimately affect an individual's quality of life. So, it makes sense that the body's reaction to the onslaught of perceived threats would have a detrimental effect on physical and mental well-being. Perceived threats trigger the exact same physiological response as actual threats, activating a fight, flight or freeze reaction. It's the constant stimulating of these stress responses that can lock some people (and others, not) in a chronic state of stress, *not the actual events that people experience*. We all react differently—some more intensely than others.

Once you begin the process of regulating your nervous system, you'll notice a gradual change in your physical and emotional well-being. You'll feel increasingly safe, spacious, and resilient. You will have more capacity to metabolize stress, and to give and receive love—all without the constant presence of a false threat response. It may sound too good to be true, but time and again, I've seen people's lives completely change when they learn to do this work.

Jeff's Story

I had a client named Jeff, (not his real name), a thirty-eight-year-old single male, who'd been working in the tech industry for fifteen years, when I first met him. Jeff consistently had problems with his boss, and the pressure from that contentious relationship had spilled over into the other areas of his life. He'd been diagnosed with anxiety and was prescribed high doses of medication to treat the symptoms. He also suffered from chronic adrenal fatigue syndrome, as well as persistent gout from poor diet.

Jeff experienced rather severe social anxiety, which stemmed from a childhood history of emotional abuse. As a child, he would isolate himself in his room to avoid the abuse. His mother hadn't consistently met his physical and emotional needs. His father was absent from his life and he had no other responsible caregivers. He grew into adulthood feeling that the world was an unsafe place where he would regularly be disregarded, ignored, or emotionally abused.

Consequently, Jeff never felt safe to engage with people. At work, he moved between getting defensive and shutting down whenever he faced criticism. Later, he'd feel ashamed of his behavior and terrified that he would lose his job. Jeff lived alone and didn't have any close friends; he used isolation as a protective mechanism, the same way he had in childhood. It was a heartbreaking existence that he desperately wanted to change.

Underneath his prickly demeanor, Jeff lived in debilitating fear of being rejected. His internal monologue went something like this: *People can't be trusted. They'll only hurt me if I give them the chance. I need to isolate myself from them. I'm only going to go to work. But even work isn't safe because I've got this stressful situation with my boss. I feel like a nervous wreck all the time. I can't tolerate it anymore. I'm overwhelmed. My body is in constant pain and none of my doctors can help me. If it's not one thing, it's another. I feel stuck and hopeless.*

Though it appeared that Jeff had a number of problems and complaints, I knew that there was one major thing at the root of his issues. Due to childhood abuse and neglect, he felt unsure of himself, and therefore felt unsafe, unwanted, and unloved. We began our work of re-establishing his connection to his Original Blueprint® by resetting his nervous system to regulate itself, so that it wouldn't misfire into a fearful, defensive response. A well-regulated nervous system allowed him to respond to uncertainty from a place of safety and resilience, even under the worst circumstances. Later, we worked on healing the younger parts of him that still felt like that little boy—isolated and afraid to come out of his bedroom.

During our sessions, I taught Jeff a series of techniques to regulate his nervous system. At the end of the very first session, Jeff turned to me and asked, "Is everybody suffering just like me?" "Many of us, yes," I answered. "Most people are desperately being driven by attempts to avoid suffering and fear and don't even know it."

Jeff shook his head in amazement. "Oh my God. That was me, too. I didn't know I was holding all that heaviness—until I wasn't."

It was an awakening for him. After a very short period, Jeff felt secure enough to go out and start making friends. He joined a social group of like-minded people and found—to his surprise and delight—that he wasn't responding to others with fear anymore. He was able to engage with more ease and authenticity. Perhaps most impactful was his decision to make a career change. Jeff went back to school to study an entirely different field that ignited his excitement and passion. Jeff completely turned his life around within a year.

While this may seem like an exceptional case, it's really not. Jeff's response is actually quite common for most of my clients. I've had people come out of their first or second session shedding tears because it's the first time they've ever felt at peace in themselves. They'd become so acclimated to fear and stress that they'd long ago stopped recognizing even the possibility of feeling alive and at peace.

Embodying your Original Blueprint® is the process of changing your beliefs and behaviors to come into alignment with your natural state. If you're showing up in a spacious and regulated body, it will alter how you experience both yourself and the world around you. In this book, we'll also focus on effective ways to change our thoughts to reflect the truth of who we are within, just as I did with Jeff. However, we begin first and foremost with the body because lasting change cannot happen without the crucial regulation of the nervous system.

I believe that the body is our culture's greatest blind spot. Often, we're taught that the mind is what we can control. The idea that emotions are held in the body, not the brain, is a foreign concept to most people. The brain can "think" an emotion but that's very different from actually "feeling" an emotion. We only *feel the sensation* of emotions in our bodies.

Grief, for example, is most commonly felt in the throat. Anxiety can be found as a constriction in the chest. Anger often erupts from the belly. Love and joy usually originate in our heart space. Safety and calm can often be felt in the chest *and* belly, and so on. Once we have enough resilience in our bodies to experience any feeling, regardless of how we assign judgment to the emotion ("good" or "bad"), that resilience gives us the strength and capacity to be courageous, to be vulnerable, to be fearless. Without constriction in our bodies, we feel expansive and centered. That spaciousness gives the brain an opening to get back to what it's intended to do in our modern world, which is to be innovative, creative, and relational.

When you make choices from your relaxed state, your relationships are transformed, and your experiences come into alignment with the truth of who and what you really are. Self-preservation, and the accompanying survival strategies, become less important than the desire to stand in your truth, stripped of the false self that defines the social roles we're all expected to play.

You can't be in fear *and* be *fully* present in your body at the same time. It's not physiologically possible for a body to do both. So, the body picks one or the other and it's going to pick the thing that seems most pressing for survival. This process is unconscious and instantaneous. People unconsciously scan any unfamil-

18

iar room, looking for whomever or whatever isn't safe. And "safe" is often what's familiar or recognizable to us; anything or anyone that is novel or different can cause a stress response in the body. When there is a perception of danger, the primitive brain hijacks the thinking brain. If the nervous system allows the primitive brain to take over, then your present self (regulated body and mind) isn't in charge.

Not only is this process of scanning for threats unconscious and instantaneous, it's also constant. Your nervous system tirelessly seeks threats. It's doing it when you enter a meeting room at work. It's doing it when you come home after a long, hard day. It doesn't matter if you're at a friend's house, sitting in traffic or hanging out down at the local bar—your threat antenna is always up. What it feels like in your body, is an uneasiness. You may feel withdrawn in social settings that don't seem familiar, end a relationship to avoid rejection or stay in a job you don't like. You may be afraid to speak up at work. If you do speak up, you might be overly polite, attempting to please others with a forced smile to avoid having tough conversations. Sometimes, you choose the opposite survival strategy through confrontation, bullying or intimidation. No matter what the survival response is, the imbalance signifies a body that is deeply afraid of being hurt, injured, or threatened.

Consciously reprogramming the nervous system is the most direct route to a coherent mind and a body that's present more often. Taking out the trash, scrubbing the toilet, arguing with our spouse, having stressful conversations with the boss—every challenging or mundane moment takes on a deeper resonance—even death and dying. Rather than adverse experiences repelling us, we find new ways to navigate them. But we only perceive these opportunities when our nervous system isn't misfiring.

This isn't to say that you're going to be happy all the time. That's not realistic. What we're talking about is giving you the tools and the permission to embrace your highest potential. We're talking about celebrating all our emotions, especially grief and anger—that it's healthy and safe to be angry sometimes, to cry or grieve or to show vulnerability.

You'll no longer be tempted to think, *I'm sorry for my tears. I'm just going to suppress my grief. Or anger is too much for me and others. I can't express this. Or I can't reach out for help. No one will understand.*

Denying and suppressing emotions only perpetuates more fear. But when you embody your authentic self, your perspective changes. If you're at a funeral, for example, it's not that you're not going to feel grief that someone close to you has died. On the contrary, there's a greater openness to feeling grief, anger, and all your emotions because the fear of being consumed by pain no longer stifles your responses. Being strong means we have the courage to feel vulnerable.

If we can be present with our grief, then we can move through it, heal, and come out the other side. Some part of society says it's not okay to cry or show vulnerability. We inherited that notion from our primitive ancestors and the animal kingdom where injury to the body can threaten the ability to survive an attack. We're told to hold it together and stay strong. These messages may be well-intentioned, but when people are in pain, repressing emotions can be detrimental to their health. If we suppress our emotions long enough, that repressed survival energy can turn inward and wreak havoc on the body's ability to fight off disease (as it did in my case). People need to be able to walk with and through grief, not deny it. The body must be allowed to feel the grace of release and let emotions flow. Only then is it possible to know freedom from fear and be able to fully delight in our natural ways of being.

Anger is another emotion that many people unfortunately consider taboo. Healthy anger is an unsung hero. Expressed fully, it's often your travel guide out of the realm of fear. It protects you, advocates for you and reminds you that what you say, matters. Far too many people have adopted an unhealthy relationship with anger. I understand why anger can seem scary, given how much rage, violence, and destruction we see in the world on the news. These are all unhealthy forms of anger that cause untold trauma by dividing families, cultures, communities, and nations. But *healthy* anger—like setting boundaries, speaking up for yourself, advocating for others—is your companion and friend. Healthy anger frees you up to boldly embrace your aliveness.

Forging a healthy relationship with all your emotions will help you in your journey back to your Original Blueprint®. Human beings were meant to have access to the full range of their feelings. Well-developed, body-oriented awareness will permit you to notice fear and tension much faster. Then, you can deal with the root causes rather than internalizing the distressing symptoms.

In this book, you'll learn how to unlock the secret code that allows the brain and body to start functioning in harmony. And, with enough practice, you'll begin to experience your Original Blueprint®.

The key to making progress with this work is the word *practice*. In Part Two of this book, you'll learn the exercises and rituals that are designed to liberate you from fear, stress, anxiety, and unresolved trauma. In Part Three, you'll learn how to integrate your experience into your life and the community where you live.

For now, in Part One, you're going to enter the discovery portion of this book, where you'll learn more about why the paper tiger exists, how your own body *and* brain have been complicit in creating it, and how you can use this book as a tool to help you find your way back to your authentic self.

You got this!

REFLECTIONS

_____

WHAT'S CLEARER?

After reading this chapter, what's clearer to you that you want to be sure and remember? Write your thoughts down here or in your personal journal:

_____

_____

_____

_____

_____

_____

_____

_____

_____

_____

❝

Our souls do not like stagnation. Our souls aspire toward growth, that is, toward remembering all that we have forgotten due to our trip to this place, the earth.

- Malidoma Patrice Somé

CHAPTER TWO

The Anatomy of Fear

If I say to you, "The world is a safe place," what's your immediate reaction?

If you're like most people, your mind starts searching for examples to disprove that statement. It might've just said back to you, "No, it's not!" In fact, all you need to do is turn on the evening news to see stories of war and violence, where human beings routinely inflict pain on one another. How can the world be a safe place when innocent people suffer this way regularly? The very idea probably sounds like wishful thinking.

But the reality is that most places in the world *are* safe. People taking violent action against each other is the exception, not the norm, which is why it's newsworthy. Countries and regions at peace in the world far outnumber places at war. Obviously, this is not to discount the painful reality of trauma survivors who've experienced violence. It's to say that the majority of people, on any given day, are not faced with imminent threats to their lives. Yet, most of us still feel unsafe in the world, to some degree. As we've discussed, this disconnect is because our nervous systems regularly misfire against *perceived* threats, which keeps us in a heightened state of fear. This notion of perceived threats is what we call a "paper tiger"—an illusion of fear.

No one likes to think that fear is driving them. But if you're not convinced that fear may be running your life, ask yourself a few questions:

- Do you ever get defensive when someone questions you at work or home?
- Can you forgive easily or do you tend to hold a grudge?
- Are you able to easily say you're sorry?
- Can you ask for what you need without hesitation?
- Do you ever get resentful of what you've done for others?
- Do you hesitate at all to have difficult conversations?
- Do you have a hard time saying "no"?
- What happens to you emotionally when you imagine losing your job?
- Have you ever stayed in an unhappy relationship for too long?
- Do you worry about what would happen to you and your family if a recession hit?
- How do you feel when you begin to see signs of aging in your body?
- How would you react if doctors diagnosed you or a loved one with a serious illness?
- Have you ever ruminated about contracting a serious illness?
- What would you do if someone bullied your child at school?
- Do you hesitate to take risks or make changes in your life?
- How do you feel when you think about death and dying?

Your heart rate may have gone up a little just reading this list of questions. It's a real-time example of your body preparing for a "threat" or "stressor" that isn't happening at the moment. It's a paper tiger!

Decoding Paper Tigers: The Nervous System Has the Key

Fear is an insidious, heat-seeking missile. We can feel deep and abiding fear in our bodies, and yet not be consciously aware that we're even afraid.

The human body has evolved much more slowly than the environment around us. Likewise, our physiological evolution has not kept pace with our cultural and technological evolution. Inside your body, your nervous system and your primitive, reptilian brain are still running the show.

Just like in ancient times, the nervous system is in constant communication with the primitive brain to determine if there are potential threats around us that need our immediate attention. *Does it feel safe for me to speak up at work? Can I have a difficult conversation with my partner about my feelings? Can I tell my parents what's going on with my grades at school?* These are all challenging—yet perfectly normal—moments in day-to-day life. But your nervous system will continue to perceive (falsely) the discomfort as a real threat to your survival until you train it otherwise.

Isabelle's Story

Isabelle (not her real name), 29, came to see me because of severe work stress. She reported chronic insomnia and panic attacks; she felt terrified that at any moment her boss would fire her. She walked into our first session with tears flowing down her cheeks, panicked and jittery. She was so emotionally debilitated that she had to request short-term disability to address the symptoms.

We began with self-regulation practices that would give Isabelle back the feeling of being safe. We worked on restoring her nervous system to recognize that, while work may be stressful, she is resilient enough to manage it through good self-care practices, her support system, and the tools we practiced in session.

Not only did Isabelle resolve her symptoms, but also by regulating her nervous system she was able to silence a host of negative self-talk and beliefs, change detrimental habits and turn her life around. Today, she's living fearlessly. She decided to quit her six-figure job and follow her childhood dream to be a travel writer. Isabelle now lives in Asia and is thriving in her new life and career.

We are much safer than our nervous systems imagine we are, which is why we need to teach our nervous systems to differentiate between perceived and real threat. A regulated nervous system keeps us in a healthy window of energy-increasing (sympathetic) and energy-decreasing (parasympathetic) balance. We know we're balanced and regulated when we can adapt to any situation—even the big stressors. Here's what that looks like:

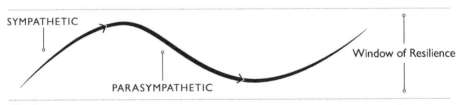

Fig. 1

WINDOW OF RESILIENCE
Feelings and reactions are viable; we can think and feel simultaneously; our reactions adapt to fit the situation.

Only situations that indicate physical danger or the potential for physical danger should trigger a survival reaction. In those cases, you need the nervous system to react instantly, using its determination of the best survival strategy for the situation—fight, flight, or freeze. Here's what it looks like when we're dysregulated, shutdown, or overwhelmed:

SIGNS OF CHRONIC HYPERACTIVATION
Emotional overwhelm, panic, impulsivity, hypervigilance, defensiveness, feeling unsafe, reactive, angry, racing thoughts.

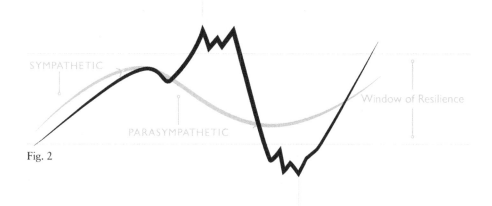

Fig. 2

SIGNS OF CHRONIC HYPOACTIVATION
Numb, "dead", passive, no feelings, no energy, can't think, disconnected, shut down, "not there," ashamed, can't say "no".

However, your primitive survival strategies just aren't appropriate for day-to-day life stressors. Stress hormones that kick in when the primitive brain activates survival strategies unnecessarily, compromise your health and limit your ability to think and respond clearly. In routine situations, you need to be spacious, well-regulated, and able to respond from your prefrontal cortex—the higher-order, thinking brain.

But, once again, how do we get there?

The Vagus Nerve: A Physical Manifestation of the Soul

We have this extraordinary nerve in our bodies called the vagus nerve. Neuroscientist and professor, Stephen Porges posits in his Polyvagal Theory, that beyond the nervous system's two main fixtures—the sympathetic and the parasympathetic—the vagus nerve brings in a third branch that stems from the parasympathetic; this branch serves to manage our social skills (e.g., communication and engagement) and helps regulate our heart rate, breathing, hearing, facial muscles, and voice. This is essential for the social aspects of thriving in life, helping us to connect with people in meaningful ways. Here's what else you should know about this super nerve:

- It connects most of your major organs to your brain (see Figure 3 for details), serving as the main line of communication between the mind and nervous system and helps regulate organs to keep you thriving.
- It's sometimes called the "love nerve" because it connects to oxytocin receptors that release the love hormone when you're connecting with your honey bunny.
- It regulates inflammation response, which strengthens your immune system's ability to fight off disease.
- It's biggest nerve bundle resides in your second brain—your gut—with 100 million neurons firing off. When people say, "trust your gut," it's those neurons signaling a message to you. We do our BEST thinking from this wise, gut-brain—also known as your "instincts".

However, the vagus nerve is not connected to our higher-order thinking brain that's supposed to be functioning on our behalf. So, until your primitive brain gets the signal from the vagus nerve that you're safe, you will continue to feel unsafe (e.g., anxious, stressed, overwhelmed) in the face of normal, everyday stimuli. When the vagus nerve is settled and relaxed, you're able to enjoy all its benefits I just mentioned and you're able to feel safe to engage your environment and the people in it.

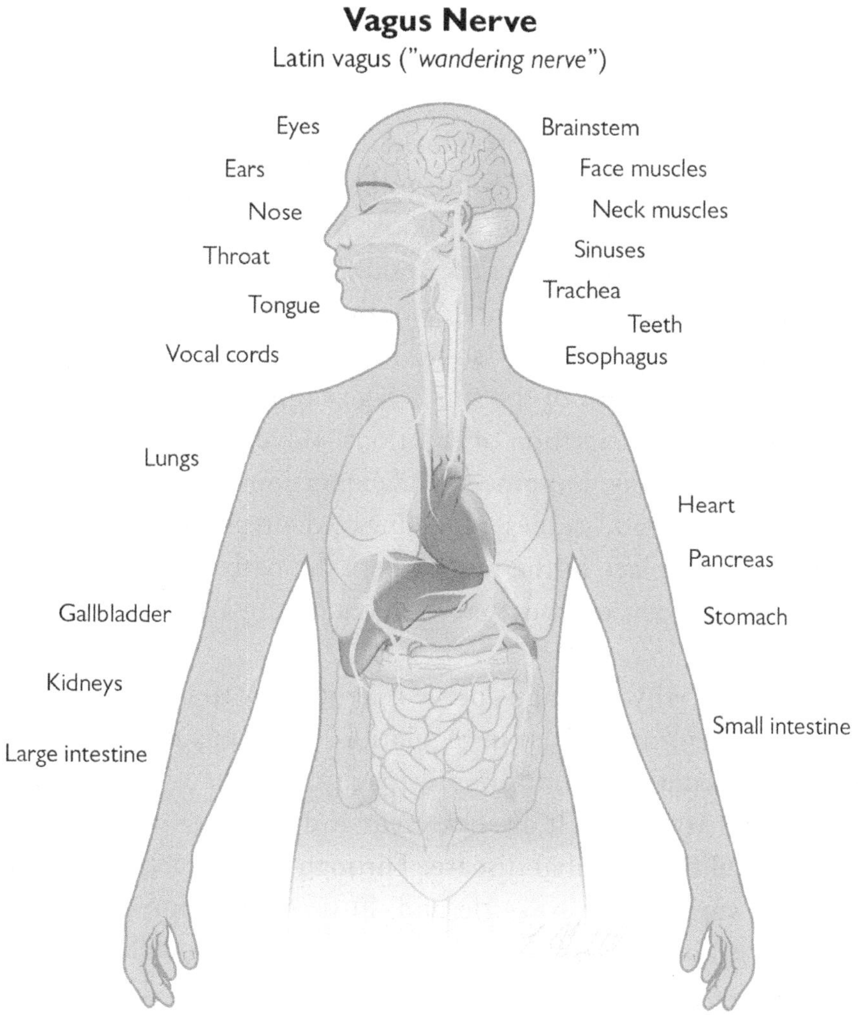

Vagus Nerve

Latin vagus ("*wandering nerve*")

Eyes
Ears
Nose
Throat
Tongue
Vocal cords
Lungs
Gallbladder
Kidneys
Large intestine

Brainstem
Face muscles
Neck muscles
Sinuses
Trachea
Teeth
Esophagus
Heart
Pancreas
Stomach
Small intestine

Fig. 3

The vagus nerve communicates with our primitive brain constantly. When you feel safe, it is because the vagus nerve releases its grip and relaxes the body's organs. When you feel a real or perceived threat, the vagus nerve constricts the normal function of these organs as part of preparation of a survival reaction (fight, flight, freeze). In these instances, you may feel tightness in your throat or chest and your heart rate may increase (pound and race) or decrease. Digestion may slow down or speed up, and breathing may increase or decrease.

These physiological responses are critical to survival. But the main tasks of the vagus nerve go beyond even these functions. Resmaa Menakem, author of the book, *My Grandmother's Hands*, astutely calls the vagus nerve the "Soul Nerve" because of its connection to our spiritual, mental, emotional, and physical well-being. Menakem has even gone so far as to call the vagus nerve, "the physical manifestation of the soul." The vagus nerve is where people experience the sensation of emotions—love, compassion, hope, joy, empathy, caring, happiness, and expansion. It's also at the seat of fear, grief, dread, sadness, loneliness, depression, anxiety, and despair. It's the place in the body where the path diverges, leading either into the den of your paper tigers or toward your Original Blueprint®.

This is why the vagus nerve is a vital key to unlocking your Original Blueprint®. When in regulation, the vagus nerve can mobilize the mental and emotional capacity to meet whatever challenge comes your way. It dissolves fear and increases your immune system's ability to combat disease. Through daily practice, you can teach the vagus nerve to settle and, in turn, communicate to the primitive brain that you're safe. The primitive brain will then open the gateway to your higher-order, thinking brain, so that you can be and feel more expansive in your everyday life.

In Part Two of this book, I'll show you simple practices to improve your body's vagal tone (optimal mental and emotional health), so that you can more deeply experience love, connection, and vulnerability—the fearless traits of your Original Blueprint®.

Jennifer's Story

When Jennifer (not her real name), 43, first came to see me, she'd had social anxiety for years and had almost given up on trying to overcome the condition. As a successful trial attorney in a law firm, she'd been working long hours for years with increasing pressure to take on bigger and more demanding cases. In the past, her performance reviews were stellar but as her stress increased, Jennifer found herself more shutdown, anxious about speaking in court cases and unable to successfully lead her team of attorneys.

Jennifer had 5-year-old, twin girls and a husband who'd been unemployed for years due to severe depression. When she came to see me, her marriage was unraveling, and she was at the end of her rope at work. She was afraid to say "no" to her boss, afraid to ask her husband and family for help, and unable to make any other changes to prioritize herself for fear her life would fall apart.

We worked on establishing boundaries at work, taking more time for self-care, building a stronger support system, and putting self-regulation and social engagement practices in place to help lower her anxiety. Over time, her performance ratings soared, she was back on her game in the courtroom and inspiring her team again.

I'll never forget the moment when Jennifer drove twenty-five miles to my office, just to come in and thank me. She cried and said, "I remember how desperate I was when we first started. The tools and practices you helped me put in place have improved everything for me. I've learned to negotiate time for myself—professionally and personally. I'm not afraid to advocate for my clients in court, lead my team and ask for more support at home. My husband and I are doing much better and my girls are happier because we are!"

Today, her anxiety has subsided and she continues to use the tools to regulate her nervous system and live more courageously every day.

The Anatomy of Fear and Loneliness

From an evolutionary standpoint, it makes sense that the human body automatically tries to conserve energy when it's in a threat reaction. If our primitive ancestors didn't have their automatic survival reactions, they would have been eaten alive and we wouldn't be here! But in today's world, there can be serious consequences when one doesn't have full access to his (or her) higher-order thinking. That's what is happening when people are under a lot of stress, they'll say that they "can't think straight." After a pulse-racing confrontation with someone, you may say something like, "In that moment, I really wanted to say X...but it just didn't come to me until later."

It's not that you draw a blank because you're not quick enough on your feet; it happens because the amygdala (the fear center of your brain) has hijacked your higher-order thinking at that moment. The circuitry is shut down. People aren't wired to have access to both parts of the brain at the same time. It's one or the other. In a fight, flight or freeze situation, the primitive brain is in charge. When you feel secure, the higher-order thinking brain is back in charge. Your goal is to regulate the nervous system to feel safe even when there's conflict, so that you can actually speak and think clearly, and have an embodied response in the moment.

Remember, this is not about avoiding fear. It's about moving with and through the fear and releasing it, so you can anchor yourself in a state of centered well-being. When you don't, the mental and emotional consequences include stress, depression, and anxiety. There can be physical consequences, as well. As doctors and researchers now know, chronic stress can suppress immune system response and create the perfect environment for disease to materialize in the body.

In my case, I know one of the reasons I struggled with cancer was because I had a lot of unprocessed fear—fear about confronting my grief, fear about my mortality, fear about my relationships and fear about my future. Those unprocessed fears had no other place to go but inside. I'm sure if you think about your own life, you'll find instances where your emotional state manifested in physical symptoms, such as a stomachache or headache or worse. This is one of the main reasons it's so important to understand the anatomy of fear and have tools to work with your emotional responses.

Isolation is a Human Epidemic

Loneliness and social anxiety are forms of fear and affect the body in similar ways. In the book, *Managing Stress: Principles and Strategies for Managing Stress,* author Brian Luke Seaward notes that 43% of adults in the US suffer adverse effects from stress. Moreover, 75 to 90% of all primary care physician visits are for stress-related complaints and disorders (American Institute of Stress). Before 1955, the leading causes of death in America were complications from infectious diseases, such as rubella or tuberculosis.

Today, statistics link stress to all the leading causes of premature death. A recent Harvard study by the "Making Caring Common" project reported that an alarming number of Americans are lonely. In the Project's national survey of approximately 950 Americans, 36% of respondents reported feeling lonely "frequently" or "almost all the time or all the time". Moreover, a startling 61% of young people (18-25) and just over half of mothers with young children reported feeling *miserably* lonely. Loneliness is linked to early mortality and a wide array of serious physical and emotional problems, including depression, anxiety, heart disease, substance abuse, and domestic abuse.

The ability to connect to others is a part of how our nervous system protects us. Evolution has designed human beings to live close to one another in symbiotic relationships. That's why few people take off for isolated areas such as Siberia or the Alaskan wilderness. The greater our number, the greater the opportunity for survival of the group *and* the individual. Conversely, when people are isolated, their likelihood of survival decreases.

Patricia's Story

Patricia (not her real name), 31, came to see me for agora-phobia (fear of public places). She was single and feeling deeply isolated in her life. Patricia's customary day consisted of working from home on her computer. Her only social contact was with her mother with whom she spoke on the phone daily. She was afraid others would judge and reject her, which contributed to fear of others seeing her.

Patricia was even phobic about coming to see me in person. I gave her practices to settle her vagus nerve; the practices engaged the social part of this nerve (eyes, ears, face, voice, throat) so that over time, social situations would feel enlivening rather than threatening. The process took time and dedication on her part but after two years, Patricia had turned her life around. She was able to leave her home, had two close friends, started a book club, and even hosted a neighborhood housewarming in her backyard.

Developing a Well-Regulated Body

Sometimes, it can be tricky to differentiate between fear-based reactions and legitimate (albeit unfortunate) realities that need to be addressed. For example, a woman abused in childhood may become hypervigilant over her own children, as a way to ensure their safety. She may restrict their movements, monitor who they can hang out with, or keep them away from family and friends. Despite her best intentions, she may inadvertently set her children up to experience the trauma of isolation and anxiety. In this case, distinguishing between a response that's warranted and one that's hyperreactive can get muddled. It's confusing when you don't understand or are not even aware of how your individual conditioning plays into beliefs, decisions, and responses.

To make these distinctions clearer, it's important to learn what it feels like to be in a regulated body. When your body is well-regulated, you immediately can tell if your words and actions are originating from an internal environment that feels secure. Regulating your nervous system means that you have clarity about real threats versus the illusion of threats. Your wise adult brain has the capacity to examine each situation and respond appropriately. So, if you're a parent having a tough conversation with your child, when you speak with love and kindness using your wise adult brain, the discussion will play out very differently than if you react from your survival strategies.

Many of us have trouble understanding emotion as sensations we feel in our bodies. We think of emotions as being more ephemeral than that. We often think of emotions as feelings that come and go. If you ask the average person, to describe their physical experience of love, for example, they might say something like, "I feel love in my chest." All emotions have a physical root in the body.

Take a moment to actually notice what you're feeling in

your body right now. What emotion is showing up? Maybe it's love. Maybe it's gratitude. Maybe it's sadness. Most likely, you'll become aware of some sensations right down the vertical line of your torso. What does the sensation of love or anger or anxiety feel like in your body? Where does it reside for you?

It's true that the sensation of love tends to reside in the heart space. Anger tends to reside in our gut. Grief gets lodged in the chest or throat. For example, I'm sure you've heard someone say something like, "He got all choked up when his close friend passed away." People can even detect danger in advance because of a feeling in the gut. I'm sure you've heard people say, "Trust your gut" or "I got this funny feeling in my gut about her and it wasn't good." We mentioned this healthy response earlier when referring to the vagus nerve and here it is again!

These aren't hard-and-fast rules and feelings may arise in slightly different areas in the body for you. The thing that's the same for everyone is the role our nervous system plays as a conduit for connection and safety. In turn, that connection improves our well-being, longevity, and sense of emotional security. When we feel safe, we have access to sensations such as love, joy, and kindness. There's a softening that happens in the body. Deep, intimate connections are possible because we feel safe. There's even a temperature change in the body. We usually don't pay attention to these subtle shifts, but you may even be noticing them as you *slow down*, reading these words. That's your vagus nerve relaxing in your body and signaling the release of oxytocin (the love hormone). It makes all the difference when you notice them, because each emotion enhances and reinforces our experience of living with a well-regulated nervous system.

When We Shutdown

Everyone has had moments where they've said to themselves, *I don't have anything left. I'm done. I'm exhausted and I've had it up to here!* It is a mental and/or emotional breakdown. There's an actual experience in your body causing those feelings. When you're under so much stress that you can't feel anything but your survival instincts kicking in, that's dysregulation.

Dysregulation is a type of activation in the nervous system. It's the feeling in the body, which says, *I don't have the space in my psychic or physical experience to tolerate anything more. I cannot take in what you're saying. I cannot listen to your feedback. I cannot hear difficult news, no matter what it is. I don't have any more to give. I'm at the end of my rope.*

When the nervous system is well-regulated, instead of feeling overwhelmed, you might say to yourself: *I'm not reacting to stressful situations. I'm able to listen to what other people have to say. Even if they disagree with me, I don't have to engage from a reactive state. I have the capacity to respond. I can respond with more creativity, kindness, and compassion, because I don't feel so overwhelmed and defensive. I'm at peace. I'm calm. I'm open. I'm relaxed.*

This is fearless living. Being fearless isn't about jumping out of airplanes or running into danger. It's about having the mental, emotional, and spiritual wherewithal to meet life with an open heart, no matter what situations arise. It's about forming deep connections to the people around us, being a benefit and a blessing to those in need and doing our part to create a world that works for everyone. It's about knowing that you have needs, that your needs matter and you can meet your needs. That sense of abundance means that you can be generous to others and willing to embrace change.

The Many Faces and Forms of Fear

All our hard, uncomfortable emotions are just fear in disguise. The average person looks at emotions such as anger, rage, grief, jealousy, spite, or sadness and sees them as separate energies that arise in response to different situations. But fear undergirds all those emotions; it all comes back to the inability to feel safe with your place in the world.

Let's take grief, for example. Grief alone, isn't what scares most people. It's the fear that if we allow ourselves to fully grieve and feel grief's full intensity, we'll die. It's the existential terror of annihilation, of falling into the abyss. So, when someone that we love dies we often lock up our feelings deep inside and refuse to look at them—sometimes for years after, if at all.

In the acute stages of grief, our bodies are designed to keep us from feeling too much pain. That's an intelligent response. People actually do die from broken hearts. We've all heard stories about older couples who've been married for many decades and when one spouse dies, the other dies shortly after. That phenomenon represents the surviving spouse giving their body permission to shut down.

From that perspective, there can be a real threat present when someone experiences such profound grief. The body can actually go into a severe stress reaction and die. The official cause of death usually is listed as some other ailment like "heart failure" or "heart attack". The emotional truth is that the person died of a broken heart, which is called cardiomyopathy.

Even though a fear of acute grief can be healthy, the answer isn't to avoid grief forever. Allowing fear to take over is never healthy. We want to feel grief but in a mindful way. Let it release on its own timeline and its own pace. No two people grieve the same way or on the same timeline.

Anger is another example. Anger is a version of the fight reaction survival energy. Some of us have been taught—for good reason—that being angry isn't safe. Women and people of color, especially, are told, *Don't get angry—smile so they stop harassing you. Don't get angry or he'll leave you! Don't get angry or you could be fired! Don't get angry or they could shoot you!*

Those thoughts and beliefs represent the nervous system saying it's not safe or appropriate to feel anger. It seems, more often than not, that it is socially acceptable for men (specifically White men, when you're talking about Western society) to get angry with a reasonable expectation that their anger won't cause imminent threat to *their* lives or livelihood. But many women and people of color sense that expressing anger could cost them dearly. A new job or a deserved promotion could disappear. Anger can cause others to judge them unfairly. And anger can—and has—cost too many Black people their lives.

Emmett Till, Martin Luther King, Malcom X, George Floyd, Breonna Taylor are a few among the countless number of Black people who've lost their lives for unjustifiable reasons that many people outside this community are just starting to wake up to. So, depending on who you are, you may shy away from expressing your anger, even when doing so would be healthy and justified.

Many women have had the experience of others telling them, "You should smile more!" While the person saying it usually doesn't intend any harm, there's an unhealthy subtext that seeks to deny women the ability to express the full range of their emotions. Tennis Champion Serena Williams once said during a press briefing when a reporter asked her why she wasn't smiling, she remarked, "Do you ask male athletes to smile during an interview?"

We should all be brave enough to tell our truth when someone wants us to do something that we don't want to do. But our culture conditions women to believe that they're supposed to smile, be pliable, passive, and non-threatening. When a woman steps out of that role, people often freak out. Sometimes smiling and laughing are defense mechanisms to stay safe in situations where women fear a backlash if they behave more freely.

But it's okay to be angry. It's okay to not smile. However, it will never *feel* okay to go against these cultural norms, unless we can regulate our own nervous systems to respond only to justified threats and not be unnecessarily threatened by each other.

Conversely, there are people who walk around furious all the time. Being enraged is different than the mindful expression of healthy anger. Examples of healthy anger include setting boundaries with people so that they know where they stand with you, advocating for yourself, and being more comfortable with conflict. When you don't express anger in a healthy way, it can fester and eventually turn into resentment. Resentment is an example of repressed anger and envy. It's toxic to you and to the people around you and will calcify in your body over time. Still, people stew in quiet resentment, rather than expressing their truth, because they don't want to "make other people mad or uncomfortable" or they don't want others to judge them. Much like grief, the anger and envy aren't what people are afraid of; it's the reaction that they fear receiving from others that's the problem. Learning to regulate your nervous system is the answer.

Shake It Off

We are the only animals on the planet who've lost our innate abilities to release fear. Fear creeps into our hearts and our thoughts in so many ways. It's insidious and sneaky. Humans no longer process fear the same way that other animals do. Other animals don't have the benefit (or the curse, depending on how you look at it!) of the brain's ability to repress fear, anger, and grief. It's remarkable how other animals respond under stress in the wild. When a cheetah chases a gazelle, if the gazelle escapes, it shakes off the fear (the activation in its nervous system) and rejoins its herd.

If a lion must defend his territory, he doesn't stop to worry what the other lions will think of him, if he gets angry. He just growls and roars to protect himself and the pride. Animals don't keep themselves from feeling anger because it's a perfectly natural response. Anger is how animals tell other animals not to cross the line—it's a way to set and hold boundaries.

When the lion protects itself, it protects its pride. And when the threat passes, the lion releases its angry posture because it has pushed back at the external threat. End of story. We humans need to re-learn how to respond this way; otherwise, our reactivity to stress and fear will compromise our well-being and our ability to find our way back to our Original Blueprint®.

Being able to mindfully experience—and then release—our more uncomfortable feelings, such as grief and anger, leaves us open to live in the moment in a way that feels safe to feel our joy and live in gratitude. This, in turn, optimizes our ability to be fearless. Your relationships will dramatically improve, because not only are you changing, but you're also changing the conditions for your interactions with the people closest to you.

When I am coming from a place of kindness and a loving heart, I'm not reactive to the things that other people say and do. Instead, I can respond without judgment. I can be spacious in my body, trusting that I'm safe. This type of engagement with others will invariably create more connection, more intimacy, more love, and deeper relationships. Innovation, creativity, and bold thinking flow from a well-regulated body. Other people will feel more comfortable confiding in you, challenging you, and being honest with you, when things aren't going well for them. You become the safe harbor, where others feel safe and encouraged to flourish. This, in turn, will enhance all your relationships and every aspect of your life.

REFLECTIONS

WHAT'S CLEARER?

After reading this chapter, what's clearer to you that you want to be sure and remember? Write your thoughts down here or in your personal journal:

_____

_____

_____

_____

_____

_____

_____

_____

_____

_____

_____

> **❝**
>
> *We now understand that trauma's imprint is both psychological and somatic: long after the events are over, the body continues to respond as if danger were ever present.*
>
> – Janina Fisher

CHAPTER THREE

How We Survive Childhood

Growing up, were you a disruptor, the rebel, the "bad" one in your family? Or, were you the good kid who always smiled and never complained? Did you dream a lot, escape through books or substances? Did you dig into every opportunity to get angry, confrontational, or demanding? Kids play roles in families to navigate their way through childhood. It's developmentally smart to do so, but as people get older some of those childhood roles can still be running the show.

I used to be a big people pleaser. I worried constantly about what other people thought of me. I feared I'd get fired for not performing up to other people's standards and I avoided confrontation as if it were the plague. I had a desperate need to be liked by everyone. This was especially true when I was working for companies in my twenties and thirties. I'd spend countless hours at work—evenings, weekends, early mornings. Often, I arrived at work before sunrise.

Most of my bosses during that period weren't tyrants—they had no expectation that I should spend that much time at work. It was me. I was desperate for their approval, and I fixated so much on my performance that I entirely neglected any semblance of a personal life. It was work, work, work. I thought, *If I can outperform everyone, then I'll be liked, get others' approval, and feel safe.* I was terrified of disapproval, so I set high standards for myself. Those entirely unrealistic expectations kept me imprisoned in a constant search for external approval.

One day something changed me. I was at work and my boss called me into her office. One of the company executives had complained about my performance. I wasn't used to getting negative feedback. The executive had told my boss that he was "deeply dissatisfied with my work and wanted to work with a different consultant." I was crushed. I immediately began to replay all the meetings and assignments the executive had given me, wondering what I had done wrong.

That's when my boss said to me, "The sooner that you can get comfortable with other people's disappointment, the less you'll be locked into trying to please anyone but yourself." In that moment, I realized that I'd spent a decade trying to please other people. Later, I realized I had been chasing the ghost of my father—desperate attempts to win his approval even though he had been long gone. My way of navigating my childhood was to avoid anger, stay small and keep the peace. I smiled, danced, and laughed my way through painful and scary moments. It kept me safe back then. But I was still using those people-pleasing strategies as an adult and it was killing me.

Talking with my boss made me realize that life would be much more satisfying if I focused on pleasing myself. That day initiated a decade-long pursuit to discover what I cared about, identify, and establish my own measures of success and focus on making myself, not others, happy first. It was my first taste of what it's like to thrive, and not merely survive.

Healing the Inner Child

The human mind processes fear in ways unique to every individual's earliest experiences and upbringing. As children, we look to our caregivers to meet our essential needs. When it seems like our caregivers will not or cannot meet our needs, children will default to primitive survival strategies to ensure their safety. Though the basic survival strategies are the same for all humans (fight, flight, freeze), people also can take on other developmental-related survival strategies, when the circumstances demand it. These survival strategies learned in youth can follow people into adulthood, even when the strategies no longer serve their best interests.

In the book, *Healing the Fragmented Selves of Trauma Survivors: Overcoming Internal Self-Alienation*, author Janina Fisher eloquently explains that the right brain remains dominant throughout childhood where, among other critical functions, survival strategies shape our reality. Children rely on these survival strategies to navigate everyday life. Meanwhile, the left brain (and corpus callosum) develops more slowly and isn't fully developed until our mid-20s.

Stressors or trauma can interrupt child development. The traumatized child self forms when a child doesn't feel safe at home. The disconnect doesn't have to be the result of a "major" trauma; in fact, the slightest disruption in our development can cause the fragmentations to form, like branches off a sapling.

The problem is that those fragmented parts of us from childhood remain on high alert for repeated danger as we age into adulthood. That's why we keep repeating the same unhealthy strategies when we get triggered as adults. Moreover, when children *do* suffer repeated or prolonged stress or trauma, the survival strategies that are automatically triggered by even subtle reminders of the trauma can obscure their self-perception—and the world around them—well into adulthood.

In describing the brain-body connection and how it relates to our ability to heal from trauma, Fisher writes:

> "We don't survive trauma as a result of conscious, frontal lobe decision-making. In the moment of life threat, our survival [reactions] are set in motion by an area in the temporal lobes called the limbic system, the repository for all our emotional, sensory, and relational experiences...We are in 'survival mode,' where pausing to think might waste precious minutes of response time. But the price of automatically engaging instinctive animal defenses [reactions] is that we lose the ability to bear witness to the entirety of the experience...
>
> As the price for our surviving the experience, then, we are left with unfinished neurobiological responses and an inadequate memory record of both what has happened and how we endured it... Worse yet, if the environment is chronically traumatizing, as are most childhood traumatic environments, the survival response system will become chronically activated, resulting in long-term effects on the developing brain and body." (www.janinafisher.com)

In other words, the primitive mechanisms that people rely on to keep them alive also block their ability to accurately process stress and trauma. Consequently, they develop various coping mechanisms in an unconscious attempt to "make sense" of what's happened. Some coping mechanisms regularly seen in trauma survivors include attachment and relationship issues, inappropriate risk-taking behaviors, re-enactment behavior, caretaking, self-sacrifice, re-victimization, and addiction.

While many of these coping mechanisms seem self-destructive, they actually represent neurobiological attempts to manage trauma by modulating a dysregulated nervous system. Some of these behaviors produce adrenaline and endorphin responses, while others numb the senses. In each case, the body is trying its very best to regulate itself and find balance in the face of overwhelming negative input.

Adapted from Fisher's work and her predecessors, I have expanded the model from the classic five instinctive survival strategies (some of which may still be running parts of your life) to include healthy examples of resilience you may be expressing in adulthood:

(see chart on following page)

WHO'S RUNNING THE SHOW?

SURVIVAL STRATEGIES	CHILDHOOD Examples of Developmental Stressors	ADULTHOOD Examples of Resilience △ NEW
FIGHT Vigilance	Resentful Judgmental Mistrustful Self-destructive Controlling/intimidating	Self-advocacy Speaking up Boundaries Trusting instincts Self defense
FLIGHT Escape	Distancing Ambivalence Addictions Eating disorders	Envisioning possibility Contingency planning Healthy distractions Escaping violence
FREEZE Immobility	Frozen Terrified Wary Phobic of being seen Panic attacks	Grief (acute stage) Stillness Waiting Listening Play dead (real threat)
SHAME Submit	Ashamed Self-esteem Passive/self-sacrificing "Good girl/boy"	Deferring to experts Admitting ignorance Getting support Complying for safety
ATTACH Cry for Help	Rescuing behavior Fearing abandonment Fearing rejection Dependency	Secure connection Intimacy/vulnerability Communicating needs Emotional honesty
△NEW **APPEASE** Pleasing	People pleasing Holding in emotions Staying small Conflict avoidance	Taking turns leading Prioritizing needs Finding common ground Good diplomacy
△NEW **SCARCITY** Deficits	Hoarding Not sharing Withholding Undermining others Not enough/not here	Budgeting Saving Abundance Appreciation/gratitude Sharing with others

Fig. 4   Adapted from: Fisher, 2017; van der Hart, Nijenhuis & Steele, 2006

First, I invite you to give yourself a pat on the back and celebrate any examples you are using from the right column—adulthood examples of resilience. Give yourself credit for all the healthy strategies you do well and know that there is no room to blame yourself if any of your survival strategies are still running you; it's natural and you have everything in you to change those strategies into resilient ones.

If you're wondering whether some childhood developmental stressors are still affecting your life, ask yourself these questions:

- Have you ever had the feeling that you're still a kid, as though there's just some part of you that doesn't feel totally grown up?
- Have you ever looked at other adults and felt envious of them because they appear to have fully functioning lives?
- Do you find yourself in unhealthy relationships with others that seem to reflect the relationship your parents had or the behavior of one or both of your parents?
- Do any of the examples listed in Figure 4 under "Developmental Stressors" still run your life when you're under stress?

Your hidden feelings may represent the places inside you that stopped growing and developing apace with the rest of your adult brain. These sentiments are common; I think that many of us harbor quiet misgivings at one time or another. Of course, there are people who've had healthy childhoods and, as adults, feel fully secure in their lives. These lucky individuals developed secure attachments with their parents (or primary caregivers). Their caregivers met these children's needs during childhood, and these children grew up feeling safe and loved in a way that created a reservoir of resilience and good faith, which serves them well in adulthood. If this sounds like you or some part of you, consider yourself blessed. But I believe that many adults have experienced some form of disruption in childhood development and, as a result, have continued to rely on unhealthy coping strategies from childhood to manage daily stressors.

Fight, Flight and Freeze

For example, if you learned primarily to use the fight survival strategy as a child, that shows up in adulthood as a personality that's angry, judgmental, mistrustful, self-destructive, or controlling.

When we escape through flight as children (running away from an unsafe environment either mentally or physically), as adults we may distance ourselves from others when we get triggered. We run away when things get tough. The propensity toward flight also shows up as ambivalence or difficulty committing to things. People with this tendency may form addictions or suffer from eating disorders.

If you used freeze as a primary survival strategy in childhood, as an adult you're likely to continue to experience the same when under stress. You may become phobic or suffer from anxiety or panic attacks. These are all common examples of how people slip into a "freeze" state.

Shame and Submit

Some psychologists, such as Dr. Fisher, argue that there's a fourth survival strategy that people use to keep themselves safe—shame or submit. When you submit to someone who's bigger and more powerful than you, what you're saying, in effect, is: *I'm not a threat. Please don't hurt me. You're in charge. I'll do whatever you say, so that I can stay safe.* When we're kids, this strategy is a very smart one when you're in an environment where it isn't safe to speak up, get angry, or question authority. When we're adults, applying these childhood strategies can be an impediment to our continued growth.

There's a lot wrapped up in shame/submit as a survival strategy. As an adult, you may find yourself always trying to be "the good girl" or "the good boy." Criticism and conflict wound you to the core. That's because submission is a strategy that traffics in self-sacrifice and self-loathing. Children tend to believe what their parents say to (and about) them; they internalize beliefs about their self-worth based on the experiences they have with their caregivers, treating parental words as the unvarnished truth. When the parents' words or behaviors are critical or judgmental, this devastates the child and buries her true, innocent self beneath layers of shame.

Submit and shame are closely correlated. The shame strategy creates a quiet, sinking feeling of worthlessness that can persist despite the external indicators of success that one achieves. In *Shattered Shame States and Their Repair*, Dr. Judith Lewis Herman states, "Shame can act as a signal of interpersonal danger and helps us to submit to a critical or dangerous person. When we feel shame, we avert our gaze, bow our heads, and collapse our spines. We become compliant, we avoid behavior that might draw attention to ourselves, and we obey the people who have power over us."

When shame becomes part of our survival toolkit, we stop making the distinction between "I did something bad" and "I *am* bad." "I made a mistake" quickly becomes "I *am* a mistake." The hallmark of shame is the belief that *I'm not good enough*. Shame keeps you from rising to your full potential. It keeps you "safe" through automatic obedience but uses hopelessness as currency; shame demands that you pay for your safety by sacrificing your healthy sense of self and your authentic voice.

Using shame/submit as a survival strategy can lead to the creation of unhealthy relationships in adulthood. You might choose a partner who thinks it's funny to routinely humiliate you in front of others. You'll stay in relationships that force you to be more compliant, because it's a way to not be seen; being invisible equates to staying safe when you've been trained to submit to authority. *I stay small to stay safe*, is the shape we can take when shame is running us.

Not only does trauma activate people's shame reaction, but also even well-intentioned messages from our external world can stimulate a similar effect in impressionable children. We've all heard some version of, *Don't ask for anything else. Just be grateful for what you have!* We've also heard the phrases, *Boys don't cry. Girls: don't be angry—smile. Don't rock the boat. Don't look a gift horse in the mouth.* These old sayings and idioms are ways that our parents tell us not to ask for too much in life. Again, these are well-meaning sentiments that are rooted in a desire to foster gratitude and humility. But sometimes they don't allow for confidence or the freedom of expression to fully take root.

Shame causes us to shrink; you feel uncomfortable with the idea of taking up more space in the world. That has an enormous impact on how you show up in life. You might not pursue the career you dream about, because you don't feel smart enough. You might not choose healthy partnerships or friendships, because you don't feel good enough. Shame causes people to limit themselves because of the false belief that they don't deserve to experience a wonderful, fulfilling life.

So, how can we make our way out of shame? One of the most common ways is to practice healthy fight/anger shown in Figure 4 under *Adulthood Examples of Resilience.*

Michael's Story

I had a client, Michael (not his real name), who lacked

self-confidence. As a boy growing up in a conservative town in the Midwest, he feared that someone would discover he was gay. Michael absorbed many messages from his small-town world that people like him were deviant. He grew up believing that he wasn't good enough and that there was something inherently wrong with him. To make matters worse, children mercilessly bullied Michael for being overweight.

His home, which should have been a sanctuary, was fraught with tension. His family was extremely religious and every Sunday the church pastor would quote scripture from the Bible that promised hell and damnation to sinners. The pastor would preach explicitly and repeatedly that being homosexual was an abomination. Over time, Michael couldn't help but internalize the message that he wasn't good enough. He felt deeply ashamed of what he saw as his "moral failing." To stay safe, he decided to make sure not to draw too much attention to himself.

As an adult, Michael came to see me because he lacked confidence at work. He was a competent employee, but he couldn't speak up or advocate for himself. During our sessions, he realized that he'd been harboring a deep self-loathing that affected not only his ability to be successful in his career, but also in his personal relationships. Michael had never been able to form healthy relationships, particularly romantic partnerships. He felt unworthy of love. The idea of exposing himself to scrutiny, of being vulnerable, was very frightening.

Michael's primary survival strategy was shame/submit. His self-esteem at work kept him from advocating for himself as he kept getting passed over for promotions. His romantic relationships were short-lived and emotionally toxic, reaffirming his low self-esteem.

We worked to regulate his nervous system and to use the higher-order, thinking part of his brain to re-parent himself. We unpacked the origins of his "not-good-enough" programming. Michael realized that he'd internalized a host of destructive messages and false beliefs throughout his childhood. With that in mind, we began to work diligently on talking to the part of himself that had been living in shame for so long.

Michael's wise adult brain entered into conversation with his younger self, which was stuck in the shame/submit paradigm. Gently, lovingly, he began to suggest to his younger self that a change was in order. In reality, Michael was incredibly kind and loving; he had important contributions to make in the world. Wise, adult Michael encouraged his inner child to trust him, so that they could integrate and move forward into a full, vibrant life.

Michael even came up with a new mantra: *I'm going for it in every part of my life. I'm going for it at work. I've got confidence. I'm capable and smart. I have important things to offer. I'm going for it in my personal life. I'm going to forge connections with people in my friendships and romantic relationships. And I'm going to go for it and taking healthy risks. I'm going to embrace my Original Blueprint® and live my life to the fullest!*

This new reality dramatically changed everything for him. Michael learned how to set healthy boundaries for himself and trust his decision-making. Soon thereafter, he got a work promotion. He learned to trust his instincts and found a healthy, happy romantic relationship with a wonderful man. They're now married and share a richly satisfying life. Michael also surrounds himself with a network of people that he considers close friends. Life is good again.

Attach and Cry for Help

Submit and shame survival strategies reflect the skewed bond between the parent and child. Instead of connection and warmth, the child may experience an intense fear of abandonment or rejection. This style of attachment is unhealthy and can result in mental and emotional difficulties in the future.

When infants form healthy attachments, they feel secure with their caregivers. They trust that those caregivers will meet their needs. This trust ultimately allows healthy independence and differentiation from our caregiver to develop over time. But without healthy attachment, a desperate need for connection, driven by the fear of abandonment, replaces trust. The child may want to depend on someone outside of him or herself, yet at the same time feel deeply anxious or ambivalent. When fear and anxiety are hallmarks of the relationship, it indicates that people don't feel safe. Anxiety and fear show up when a child hasn't formed secure bonds with primary caregivers.

Insecure attachment can result from one parent (or both) not being present. It can be the result of severe trauma, such as physical or sexual abuse. However, the trauma doesn't have to necessarily be severe. Sometimes, people can form insecure attachments because of seemingly simple things, such as parents having to work long hours. Perhaps a single parent was too exhausted to care for the needs of a child after she dragged herself home from work at night. Consequently, the child grew up feeling that he or she couldn't trust or rely on others.

In such cases, there's no intentional neglect. The parents are doing what they need to do to provide for the family. But the child may still form the unconscious belief that his parents' absence is, in some way, tied to the child's own lack of value (e.g., "They'd be around more if I were important.")

Sometimes a person who lacks secure attachments can grow into a fiercely independent adult. These people can run companies, travel the world, and take risks, because they rely on a powerful internal compass to guide them. The shadow side of this positive aspect is that a strong, autonomous personality can also have difficulty developing intimacy with others; it's hard to trust or count on others, if you have no practice with anyone but yourself in meeting your needs.

Louise's Story

Louise (not her real name) was a young woman who had never experienced healthy, secure attachment with the caregivers in her life, particularly her father, who was absent in her childhood. Because she didn't have a healthy father figure for a role model, she wasn't able to reference any male figures to help her feel secure around men. The job of our parents—particularly fathers—is to help us feel protected and safe. Unfortunately, Louise didn't get that security from her father, emotionally, financially, or otherwise.

Adult Louise formed unhealthy relationships with men. She tended to gravitate towards men who were unavailable, just like her father. But she was never comfortable in her relationships and would experience states of high anxiety and fear. These unhealthy patterns eroded all the connections that she attempted to form.

When she had the chance to create relationships with healthy, reliable men, she couldn't bring herself to accept their attention. Yet, she couldn't resist the charms of married men or men who lived far away from her who were only interested in short-term, no-strings-attached affairs.

As a child with an absent father, Louise had grown accustomed to feeling like she didn't matter to the men she cared about. They were always "too busy" for her. She felt like an afterthought. But she kept going back because their behavior played right into her fears of abandonment and rejection. She alternated between saying, *Don't leave me* and *Get away from me. I'm going to end this before you do.* For Louise, being vulnerable felt terrifying.

When Louise came to me, we worked very hard on helping her feel safe in her body. The feeling of safety was foreign to her. Using her wise, adult brain, she asked herself these questions: *How do I help the scared child within me feel safe without being dependent on a man? How can I create that feeling of safety for myself?*

Part of Louise's quest to create a renewed sense of self-love included facing the trauma of her past, which was the cause of her unhealthy behavioral patterns. In addition to the painful dynamic that she endured with her father, Louise disclosed to me that she'd been a target of sexual assault. No wonder she had no idea how a healthy relationship looked! No wonder she didn't understand what it felt like to feel safe in her body. She didn't know how to make choices that would uplift and edify her.

Louise had to learn to re-parent herself, to find ways to meet her own needs, rather than struggle to get those needs met by toxic people. Louise deconstructed her entire relationship paradigm, ultimately re-learning how to accept help and support in healthy ways while taking pride in meeting her own needs.

Louise realized that one of her underlying beliefs was that she needed to date unavailable men because that was her way of seeking to repair her parental relationship. That's what we do: We recreate the kinds of relationships we experienced growing up—even if they were extremely unhealthy—so that we can "repair" the original attachment rupture. But that almost never works. The survival strategies that we bring with us from childhood retrigger us without moving us any farther along the path toward healing. We gravitate toward the familiar until we learn otherwise.

Over time, Louise began healing her traumas rather than just recreating them. She learned how to recalibrate her nervous system to feel safe, while re-parenting herself in a loving and healthy way. She discovered that her Original Blueprint® was a strong, capable, confident woman who could meet any challenge and open herself up to love.

Appease

I've added two more survival strategies to the mix—appease and scarcity. A cousin of submit/shame, appease is an attempt to show that you're non-threatening. Girls, for example, are warned to be nice and ladylike under all circumstances. They're rewarded for being overly polite to others.

People of color also use appease to demonstrate that they are non-threatening to White people. It's a survival technique that's intended to protect people in situations where they feel like they can't be fully transparent or express themselves honestly. There are innumerable examples of people of color speaking up (in a way that a White person wouldn't hesitate to do) only to find their life in danger. This strategy can be a surprising blind spot for White folks, if they haven't been exposed to the great divide in cultural perspective and experience.

Appeasing is about keeping the peace, deference, and not raising issues that could stimulate an adversary to attack or take a threatening stance. Sometimes this strategy works and sometimes it doesn't. But what it always does is prevents people from having honest dialogue with one another. You don't really know where you stand with people who appease. They can't be honest because they're afraid of the conflict that might ensue.

Jennifer's Story

Jennifer (not her real name) came to see me in her 30s because she'd been sexually molested by a close family friend for nearly a decade, beginning when she was just nine years old. After exploring her family history, we talked about how the perpetrator groomed her and controlled her to create the conditions where he could abuse her without fear of repercussion.

Jennifer grew up in a home where both parents taught her that it's important to be nice to people. *Smile! Please others. Don't rock the boat. Don't confront people or discuss difficult topics. Keep it light. Keep it nice.* From as early as she can remember her parents conditioned her to appease others. That was the reason she never told her parents about the perpetrator. This "friend" came to all the family events and gatherings. He was there for Christmas and Thanksgiving dinners, smiling and laughing, gaining her family's trust. Eventually, as she grew older, Jennifer's wise adult brain started to come online, and she began to see clearly that maintaining her silence wasn't healthy. What happened to her wasn't just and it wasn't her fault.

"He'd been brainwashing me all these years to stay quiet," she said. "I can't stay quiet anymore."

But speaking up proved to be difficult. A part of Jennifer had internalized deep shame that she coped with by appeasing and pretending everything was ok. Her parents taught her that anger was bad and dangerous—to shy away from difficult topics so that other people wouldn't feel uncomfortable. Obviously, that created the perfect conditions for the perpetrator, because Jennifer felt she could never tell her parents. *"You tell them, and they'll be angry,"* he said. *"You don't want them to be angry, right?"* As a young child, she believed him, so she kept quiet. In her innocence, Jennifer believed that she was to blame.

Once we identified Jennifer's survival strategies of appease and shame, we worked with self-parenting exercises to help her see that she held no responsibility for what happened. The shame belonged with her perpetrator only. Once she internalized that she wasn't to blame, she was able to access healthy anger. Her anger enabled her to set clear boundaries, to be a strong advocate for herself and to speak her truth. She practiced being honest and open, and finding ways to become comfortable confronting people when necessary. For the first time, she recognized how toxic and destructive the old patterns of appease and shame were for her.

As a result of our discoveries, Jennifer made drastic changes in her life. She finally disclosed to her family the years of sexual abuse that she'd endured. The family shunned the molester and immediately reported him to the authorities. Jennifer found a renewed sense of confidence, as she learned to use the power of her voice for the first time in her life.

Life is a work in progress. Jennifer continues to do the practices to regulate her nervous system, allowing her to feel safe in her body. She's in a far better place—confident and free to express herself openly. She started her dream job, bought her own home, and found a healthy relationship.

At the end of our work together, she said, "I'm my own hero now."

Scarcity

The other survival strategy that I've added is scarcity. Scarcity is deficit thinking; it's the belief that there's not enough to go around. Someone suffering from a scarcity mindset might say: *Focus on yourself. Don't share what you have. Take what you need. This place is ours: Outsiders aren't welcome!* The scarcity mentality keeps people from being kind and generous. It limits one's ability to see another person's perspective.

Children who face intense deprivation may fear for their survival. As adults, that fear can transform into the desire to hoard money, food, or possessions. At work, they may refuse to share their expertise or provide help to co-workers. They may even try to sabotage other people's efforts because they're afraid that someone else will outshine them. People who suffer from a scarcity mindset perceive threats around every corner. They usually feel fearful and insecure about their own competence. It all originates from an intense fear that there aren't enough resources available for everyone to have what they need to survive.

If you see the world as unsafe, it makes sense that you'd want to hold onto as much as you can. But the perception that there isn't enough to go around is simply false. On the contrary, abundance means there's plenty to go around. Life is full of exponential possibility.

Your survival strategies play a very important role in keeping you safe. But life is not just about surviving; it's about thriving and savoring your precious time here on this planet. It's about living a life of purpose. When we over-use or mis-use old survival strategies, they stop serving their evolutionary function. Instead, they hold you captive in a lifetime of fear. You're not able to maintain healthy relationships with people when you're coming from a fragmented, younger child self. Being trapped in that cycle causes more isolation and fear.

The good news is that you don't have to live like this. You have an amazing, wise adult brain and body that can step into the foreground of your life. No longer do you need to let your survival strategies run the show. When you use the tools that you'll learn in Part Two of this book, you can begin to re-parent and integrate the parts of yourself that need healing.

No one could heal you better than you.

When the nervous system is regulated and the higher-order, thinking brain is fully functioning again, they forge a relationship within the body that is much healthier than simply leaving the primitive brain and a dysregulated nervous system to run the show. Only then can you scale back your reliance on your old survival strategies that may have kept you safe in the past, but that now inhibit your growth and endanger your ability to thrive and flourish.

REFLECTIONS

WHAT'S CLEARER?

After reading this chapter, what's clearer to you that you want to be sure and remember? Write your thoughts down here or in your personal journal:

_____

_____

_____

_____

_____

_____

_____

_____

_____

_____

> *If you want to go quickly, go alone. If you want to go far, go together.*
>
> - African Proverb

CHAPTER FOUR

It Takes a Village

So far, we've been talking about how our experiences in life shape us as *individuals*. But we aren't alone—we need each other to thrive. So, it's equally important to ask for help and seek opportunities to support others. In the end, everyone shares the same sacred responsibility to help others, whether we recognize and accept that responsibility or not. Reciprocity is key to our existence. It's as integral to our survival as our very breath.

How good are you at *giving* to others? How good are you at *receiving* from others? The balance of both is essential. Our global village is one big organism. When one person suffers, that suffering has a ripple effect, just like a rock dropped into the water ripples outward. For example, how can a virus spread across the world so quickly? It's because people are interconnected. The same is true for how people's nervous systems ping off each other.

Just think about how you feel after you've fought with a

loved one, read a doom-and-gloom news story or watched an intense movie. These activities likely trigger your nervous system in some way—causing anger, frustration, overwhelm, heartbreak, sadness, denial, etc. People deeply affect each other. If I'm regulated, I can help encourage regulation within you. When I heal, you heal. That's a phenomenon called *co-regulation*. But if I'm dysregulated and suffering, the opposite is true, too.

Togetherness—not Otherness—is a Remedy for Global Healing

Human beings have an infinite capacity to be kind, generous and supportive of one another. When that happens, I call it the *huddle effect*. It often occurs when people need support during a crisis. Suddenly, we realize how much we need each other. Recently, my neighborhood experienced a massive blackout—our public utility shut off all electricity for a week to lessen the potential for fire outbreaks during California's drought season. When that happened, my next-door neighbors turned on the only generator in the neighborhood and hosted a big dinner party. Everyone came together to break bread and enjoy each other's company. We laughed and caught up on our lives, forgetting about the blackout, joking about the minor inconveniences of no electricity, and feeling the support of our little village. We set aside political and other differences; we found comfort and support in each other's company.

Human beings need each other. We're pack animals who thrive in close contact with others. If you exist only for yourself, you risk losing out on one of the most meaningful aspects of the human experience—belonging. Being part of something larger than yourself is meaningful, fulfilling, and rewarding. It's a primary reason that people have children, impactful careers and/or an abiding faith in a higher power.

The extended village provides the familial and societal context for your core belief systems. A loving, healthy village fosters life-affirming values. Kindness, consideration, and a healthy respect for others (both inside and outside the group) are common hallmarks of a healthy ecosystem within a group. Conversely, a village where the members have suffered prolonged deprivation, separation or mistreatment can become a breeding ground for fear and mistrust.

When we find ourselves struggling with the effects of collective trauma—whether it's hardship that we've experienced firsthand, or something that's been passed through the generations—a healthy support system is one of our frontline defenses. Creating and sustaining a healthy system allows us to build the psychological bridge from fear to love.

Not only do human beings need each other for mental and emotional sustenance, but also our nervous systems depend on each other for safety and connection. When you're separated from your village, when you're lonely or isolated, there's a dramatic impact on your physical and emotional health. This isolation severely compromises your well-being. That's why people seek companionship and support from others.

The benefits of social engagement are astounding. It simply makes people healthier. Being an integral part of a social, support system reduces the effect of chronic stress on your body dramatically, because being in community reduces the production of the hormone called cortisol—the stress hormone. Belonging reduces your risk of heart disease and cancer, while increasing your immune system's resilience. Your brain works better because you're not stuck in survival mode. When you're part of a healthy community, you can feel safe again. Functioning from the higher-order, adult brain increases the capacity to engage in meaningful conversations with others, to listen without judgment, to seek understanding and solidarity in service to the greater good.

It becomes much easier to learn from others when you can abandon defensiveness and negative social conditioning. Proceeding in any interaction with curiosity and an open heart will create the space to learn from other people's experiences without feeling overwhelmed or threatened. Social support contributes to your growth and evolution and better enables you to thrive in your relationships.

In her book, *The Village Effect,* Susan Pinker refers to a 2010 study that examined close to 150 longitudinal studies about relationships and mortality. The researchers re-examined the journals of more than 300,000 study participants over the course of more than seven years. They reviewed this material and concluded that people who were fully integrated and connected to their communities had *half* the risk of dying compared to those who lived solitary lives, during that seven-year study. Proximity—meaning regular, face-to-face contact with others—is what helps people thrive and keeps them from feeling lonely.

Longevity is largely determined by your interactions with people who are in closest proximity to you. Your next-door neighbor, the people in your office, the barista you order coffee from in the mornings—the people you're in communication with on a regular basis—may be more necessary than even your relatives. You have a higher chance of longevity if you're in daily contact with people in your extended circle. Pinker argues convincingly that, "face-to-face contact is crucial for learning, happiness, resilience and longevity." Moreover, she states that, "Social isolation is the public health risk of our time." Taken from Pinker's book, this chart (Figure 5) shows its significance along with other important factors for longevity:

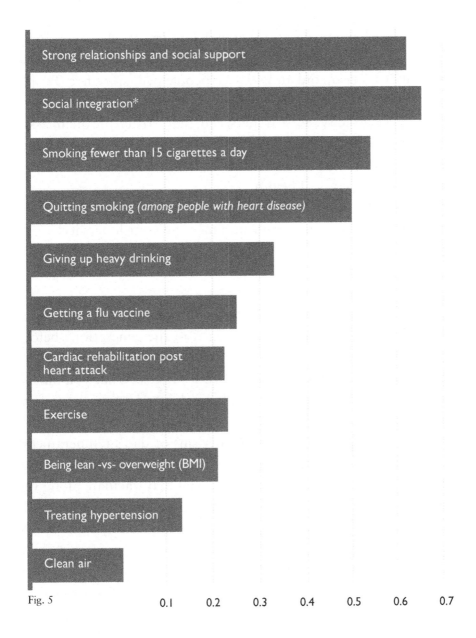

Fig. 5

Strong relationships and social support

Social integration*

Smoking fewer than 15 cigarettes a day

Quitting smoking (among people with heart disease)

Giving up heavy drinking

Getting a flu vaccine

Cardiac rehabilitation post heart attack

Exercise

Being lean -vs- overweight (BMI)

Treating hypertension

Clean air

0.1   0.2   0.3   0.4   0.5   0.6   0.7

Adapted from Pinker 2015; Holt-Lunstad 2010
*Social intergation refers to social involvent on multiple levels

According to the US National Library of Medicine, lone-liness is a very common condition affecting up to 80% of people under eighteen years old and 40% of people over sixty-five. People can feel lonely or isolated following a bereavement or after relo-cating to a new city. Researchers call that "reactive loneliness." However, as high as 15-30% of the population experience chronic loneliness, which can have serious consequences for our mental, emotional, and physical health.

Don't wait for a crisis—find time to get support from your neighbors, support your village and increase your longevity!

Inheriting the Past

You are hundreds of thousands of years old.

You carry all that has happened to the generations before you in your DNA. You hold your lineage in your cellular struc-tures, your tissues, your blood, and your organs. What you inherit is beyond eye color, hair texture, skin color and gestures. You in-herit more than markers for different conditions or diseases. You inherit even more than mom's mannerisms or dad's temperament. You also inherit the trauma from the generations that came before. Depending on your level of resilience, you may vacillate along the spectrum of surviving to thriving. The more intergenerational suf-fering your body holds, the more challenging it can be to freely move through life.

Humankind hasn't always been *kind*. Our unconscious, evolutionary bias towards fear or negativity often causes us to no-tice differences between us as a threat rather than seeing that we're each valuable, extraordinary, and unique contributions to the hu-man race. When trauma and suffering intertwine, it can create deep and often impalpable feelings of fear, shame, and regret. Collective trauma happens across families, villages, and cultures. Intergen-erational trauma is our collective trauma, passed down from one generation to the next.

If such traumas continue to transmit across generations, it becomes historical trauma. Often, we begin to see the byproducts of trauma as part of the cultural fabric of a group of people, rather than part of their trauma history. When trauma becomes too much to bear, the nervous system will attempt to protect the body by repressing the associated emotions and/or projecting historical trauma onto others, thereby creating divisions between groups of people.

Separateness can stoke the flames of animosity and mistrust. People highlight otherness instead of togetherness; they exclude rather than include. No one can find common ground when they can see only polarities—Us versus Them, Black versus White, male versus female, Democrat versus Republican. People isolate and divide. In doing so, they create the conditions to perpetuate the transmission of trauma from one generation to the next. Then, in order to survive, people develop coping mechanisms that become integral to that sub-culture. Suffering loses its context and becomes a cultural norm.

This process can have negative consequences, but many positive things can result as well. For example, a result of world-wide marginalization, abuse, ostracization, and discrimination has been the emergence of a fiercely resilient LGBTQ+ (Lesbian, Gay, Bisexual, Transgender, Queer+) culture. The community and its many sub-communities have honed self-advocacy, pride, and humor to overcome obstacles. Their shared experience of suffering over time has helped shape a culture of solidarity.

Within Black culture, the arts have long been a prominent driving force. To survive the catastrophic conditions many Black people endured during slavery, people would sing in the plantation fields and later, in the churches. Singing and faith served—and continue to serve—as coping mechanisms to find ways to survive the horrors of slavery and beyond.

Gospel hymns such as *Wade in the Water*, *Go Down Moses*, and *Swing Low Sweet Chariot*, communicated messages about escaping the plantations through the underground railroads. Drawings in the fields served as safe ways to communicate escape routes. From those early experiences, emerged whole genres of music, art, poetry, and literature. Such exquisite artistry across the many genres is now an integral part of Black culture.

Black Americans have also had a dramatic and powerful influence on American culture overall. Many of our great American patriots who've shaped our cultural values and changed the course of human civil rights have come from the Black community. It's difficult to name an aspect of American culture that hasn't been significantly influenced by Black culture. Somehow, people lost reverence and appreciation for these contributions, even as the systemic trauma of slavery lives on in the bodies of our Black friends and neighbors.

It doesn't have to be that way. When we interact with someone who appears different, our bodies can go into a stress response. To overcome that response, you need to repeatedly expose the nervous system to the same stimuli so that the system recognizes that "different" is simply "neutral" or "positive" as opposed to stressful or threatening. Microaggressions often cause repeated stress responses for people of color, compromising the body's ability to fight off stress and disease. Ultimately, the repeated exposure to such stress responses can also contribute to early death for some.

Manifesting a Global Purpose

Imagine if everyone committed a small part of their lives to healing the collective? If we felt connected to each other and understood that my wounds are our wounds (and vice versa), my suffering is our suffering (and vice versa), my history is our history (and vice versa). Would we treat each other differently from this awareness? Can you imagine the change that would happen in our global village, if people were more aware of their individual impact on others?

Imagine a world where you embraced, celebrated, and savored every interaction you had with those around you. Imagine appreciating each other's histories more, celebrating each other's contributions to the world, and speaking to each other with loving kindness. You'd care deeply about people whether you knew them personally or not. You'd acknowledge and value difference. Being challenged or corrected wouldn't be seen as a threat, but rather an avenue for greater growth and shared understanding. Repeating positive experiences with differences is how we get there; we replace the paper tigers associated with "different" for an appreciation of them.

Imagine that making a change in your life could have a butterfly effect on the rest of the world, restoring our collective resilience. What a beautiful gift that would be. To change a system, all it takes is one determined person to disrupt the status quo.

The goal of this journey is to release unhealthy survival strategies so that you can reside in your adult brain and regulated body—the seat of your Original Blueprint®. But making that transition isn't just important for your own self-empowerment—it changes how deep and meaningful your impact can be within the local and global villages. Being in the fullness of your Original Blueprint® gives you the power to ignite your global purpose.

Appreciating Differences Repairs Broken Bonds

When your bathtub has leaky plumbing, it's important to repair the leak before the whole house floods. If you ignore it, you'll have a much bigger mess on your hands. Life is like that, too. You can't ignore your wounds (or my wounds) forever without feeling the consequences. So, how do we repair the village so that it's once again a resilient, thriving global community?

You can start by examining your own views about difference. Do you value what each person brings to the world? Do you truly understand that how you treat others—implicitly or explicitly—matters? Can you appreciate that you may have blind spots that lead you to the conclusion that your experience is the same as others?

Take, for example, the Aboriginal people in Australia who have a 50,000-year-old relationship with their land. This tribe can feel the grass and know if it will burn well; they know the types of fires to burn for what type of land, how long and how frequently it needs to burn to prevent larger fires from erupting. The complexity of this knowledge has been difficult for Australian firefighters to replicate when combatting forest fires. Without this kind of complex intergenerational knowledge to call upon, the damage brought on by climate change has proven to be even more difficult to overcome.

Many Western cultures have not understood or appreciated many thousand-year-old traditions such as these. Our lack of appreciation has led the collective to suffer around the world. Much like with the Aboriginal people in Australia, there are similar situations where North American colonialism largely has wiped out or disenfranchised indigenous cultures. Such loss has caused the degradation of essential knowledge about humankind's relationship with the earth, among other things. We know one of the consequences of that lost wisdom—the tragedy we now experience with fire seasons that are ravaging the Western United States.

Small changes can add up to something big, too. You might reflect for a moment about the cultures in your village who've been neglected or under appreciated. What could you do to change that? For example, is there a business you can frequent more that's owned by someone outside your culture? Could you tutor a student from another culture in a topic you know well? Maybe volunteer at a community garden? Visit a place of worship different from your own? You can visit art exhibits that highlight other cultures, join a club that emphasizes diversity or check out humanlibrary. org to talk with someone different from you about a topic of interest.

Only paper tigers believe that differences are dangerous. In reality, differences are not only beautiful, they're also important. Every culture, and every person within the culture, has a part to play in the evolution of our species. We need everyone on board.

Need to take a break? If you do, stand up and take a nice, deep breath before you continue.

Taking Responsibility

As adults, we have a responsibility to contribute to our communities, especially once we've done our own healing work and can bring our wholehearted self back into the community. We must be open to the reality that everyone's experience is not the same. To support a healthy village, we can seek to understand how our behavior impacts other people.

You can't live a life of integrity, if you behave one way toward your family members or the people in your "group" but treat other people differently. Part of embodying your Original Blueprint® has to do with standing in your integrity. When I'm standing in my integrity it means that I honor my values the same way in every situation and every scenario. I'm no different when I'm at home than I am at work or when I'm with friends or when I'm with my partner or when I'm talking to the bus driver or the neighbor down the street. I interact with others as the same integral person—respectful, curious, open, and unafraid.

Living in integrity, without fear manipulating your thoughts and decisions, offers you a chance to look at your own impact on the world. You can choose to embrace your personal responsibility to give back to your community in ways that benefit everyone, not just yourself or those closest to you. Connecting with people who are different from you requires stepping out of your comfort zone. But if you're able to get curious about how life is different for other people, you'll learn so much more about how you fit into the larger scheme of things. And you'll be better able to answer the question: *What can you do to help support others as they step into their full potential?*

Social Impact

Intergenerational trauma and learned biases, combined with the morals and values that you inherit from your village, influence the way you perceive every aspect of life. Your social conditioning affects everything from gender roles to leadership opportunities to your parenting style. It influences where you work, how you live, and whom you love.

Human beings are socially conditioned to seek safety and we do that by adhering to cultural norms of our society because we want acceptance. But what happens when social conditioning is harmful to us or others, as is the case with social ills such as institutionalized racism, gender discrimination or class bias? What happens when your social conditioning tells you that you aren't fit to live the life that you dream of? What do you do if your social conditioning tells you that, for example, people who look different are enemies or that someone else's religion is wrong or that women are inferior? How can you use what you've learned about living authentically to step out of that destructive conditioning?

You can have a tremendous impact in the world as a leader, parent, partner, or community member, when you practice your ability to objectively distance yourself from adverse or reactive conditioning. When you're not coming from a place of fear anymore, you can muster the courage to look at how you've impacted your village. If that impact has been harmful, you can take personal responsibility to make meaningful changes.

For example, if I'm a CEO of a company, I'm empowered to listen, get informed and then take responsibility for where I may be holding implicit biases. I can change who I hire, develop, and promote people, how I provide growth opportunities to team members, how I represent the organization, and how I collaborate with my peers. There are ways in which I can begin to bring my unconscious thoughts and actions into the forefront of my conscious mind. Then, the choices that I make begin to shift the entire culture of my organization to ensure that our corporate system is really working for everybody.

If I'm a parent, I can empower myself to look at how my fears and conditioning have shaped my interactions with my child. I can be honest with myself about what kind of messages I'm passing along to him or her. What survival strategies have they developed to cope with the environment that they're living in? Am I passing my prejudices and traumas down to my children, causing them to see the world from a skewed lens? Am I expecting my kids to heal my own wounds?

If I can answer these questions honestly, without defaulting to anger, denial, shame, or self-blame, I can create the opportunity to become a more conscious parent. Think about what it would mean to raise children who see the world as a safe and loving place, where there is more than enough to go around for everyone. That perspective would give them more choice about how they respond, when faced with the inevitable challenges that life brings. It would give our global village a chance to restore itself in the generations to come. The most influential job in the world is being a parent.

The Power of Spiritual Practice

Throughout history, one of the most powerful points of connection for human beings has been the ritual observance of some form of spiritual practice. The vastness of the universe—and the precariousness of our place in it—can amplify feelings of loneliness and separation. As we have seen, lack of connection heightens fear reactions and diminishes virtually every aspect of life, including longevity. Connecting to a higher power, and to other like-minded people in faith-based communities, creates powerful bonds that give life meaning and purpose.

There are many different lenses through which to interpret and enjoy spirituality. I take no position about the efficacy of one belief system over another. Instead, I define spirituality as being connected to something within or outside of the Self that has infinite capacity, wisdom, and love at its root. Infinite capacity is something that is far more expansive than what our social communities can provide.

So, you may choose to engage (or not) in contemplative practices such as mindfulness, meditation, prayer, walking or journaling. Being out in nature may provide you with the sense of spiritual union that you crave. You can also be part of a community at a church or temple, synagogue, or mosque. Or you may choose not to be part of any kind of organized religion. The point is to be in a relationship with a higher power that can provide an infinite container for your growth and healing.

More specifically, spirituality is an important way that you can support your body's healing as you return to your Original Blueprint®. When you feel connected to something bigger than yourself, your nervous system functions better because you feel safe and more regulated. Blood pressure lowers. You sleep better and longevity and well-being increase. It is from embodied states that we can heal and create balance in our physiology. Studies have even shown that people who have a regular mindfulness or meditation practice have a far lower risk of depression or anxiety.

The great Sufi mystic Rumi once wrote, "Don't feel lonely.

The whole universe is inside of you." It's a beautiful reminder that you're never alone. If you have a connection to your creator, to the universe, to nature, to God—however you describe your higher power—you have access to a whole world nestled in the core of your own being. You can feel a sense of fullness when you're connected to it, which supports you in your quest to gain mastery over fear and return to your Original Blueprint®.

Please keep in mind that when I use the phrase "spiritual practice," the critical word is practice. To get all the benefits I've mentioned, it's imperative to couch your belief system inside regular practices that keep you connected to your Infinite Source, yourself, and your community.

Ritual is key to our individual and collective healing. Whether it's being with others or going to a place of worship or taking hikes with friends or even inviting your neighbors over for dinner, developing rituals of communion will not only heal you but it will help heal your village.

❝

Don't feel lonely. The whole universe is inside of you.

- Rumi

REFLECTIONS

WHAT'S CLEARER?

After reading this chapter, what's clearer to you that you want to be sure and remember? Write your thoughts down here or in your personal journal:

_____

_____

_____

_____

_____

_____

_____

_____

_____

_____

Get the Companion Workbook @ IrisInstitute.com

Before you begin Part Two, I highly recommend you download the *Companion Workbook* from my website, IrisInstitute.com where you will also find the book's worksheets, video and audio recordings of the exercises and rituals, and other helpful materials.

If you decide not to take advantage of these resources, be sure to have a personal journal dedicated to Parts Two and Three exercises and rituals.

Transitions: Part One to Part Two

As you may know, anytime you transition from one experience to another, it's important to re-set for the upcoming experience. Whether you're making a simple transition (such as going from the office to home, moving from one meeting to the next, etc.) or contemplating much bigger transitions (like changing careers or moving to a new city), staying in the present moment as you prepare to move ahead means that you will do so from your embodied, authentic self. Take a deep breath. Notice what's different for you already.

It's time to step forward.

CONGRATULATIONS!!!

You are well on your way :)
Keep up the outstanding work—you got this!!!

PART
TWO

RECLAIMING BALANCE

❝

Authenticity is a collection of choices that we have to make every day. It's about the choice to show up and be real. The choice to be honest. The choice to let our true selves be seen.

- Brené Brown

PART TWO

Reclaiming Balance

Introduction: How to Practice

In an ideal world, you'd learn from early childhood to embrace all that is wonderfully unique about yourself. You'd understand that you're so much more than a collection of your mistakes. You'd receive unconditional love—cherished and celebrated in your defeats as well as your successes. You would recognize that the world is filled with people who share the same desire to be seen and accepted, to love and be loved. You'd learn to regulate your mind and body, so that you could quickly return to your natural state of equilibrium when faced with difficult experiences, and revel in experiences that delight you. In short, you'd learn to tame your paper tigers so that you could flourish in the peace and safety of your Original Blueprint®. This would be the natural course of your evolution.

As it stands, however, very few of us got the training to make the mental and emotional journey into wholeness. But if you believe what I believe—that every experience we have in life happens by design—it becomes easier to recognize that there are no mistakes. Mistakes are ways that the soul grows. Embrace them as opportunities for deeper learning. Each time you overcome something, you're taming your fears and moving closer to your Original Blueprint®.

In Part Two, you will learn more about embodying your Original Blueprint®: how to decode your fear anatomy; how to understand and repair the survival strategies you used in childhood; and how to rely on your support systems to increase your well-being and longevity.

Exercises, Rituals, and Levels

Throughout Parts Two and Three, you'll notice two words used repeatedly—*exercises* and *rituals*. **Exercises** are meant to be done **once** or **twice**. **Rituals,** on the other hand, are meant to be **repeated.** It's important to understand the difference, so that you can identify what requires repetition and what doesn't. You will also see that there are three distinct levels for each of the exercises or rituals, each noted with one to three icons: Beginning, Intermediate, and Advanced.

Rituals are *repeatable practices* that help to change or rewire your brain's neural pathways and your body's neurophysiology. Rituals are essential for change—the more you repeat a ritual, the more it becomes your new way of being. For your muscle memory to integrate a ritual, you need to repeat it 300 times. If you repeat it 3,000 times, you embody the ritual. It becomes the new and natural way you live your life. That's when your fears, stressors and setbacks no longer impede your ability to thrive. You can then experience a surge in quality of life for yourself, your children, and grandchildren because you have fundamentally changed.

Here's a metaphor to help you envision what I'm talking about: Imagine a mountain with paths that wind up the mountainside, all the way to the peak. The pathways have been worn down over the course of many, many years. There are certain pathways that people travel regularly—habitually—until travelers no longer need maps and signs to point the way. Some parts of that path towards the mountain's peak are safe and healthy for you. But you'll also run into slippery areas that can cause injury, rendering the path unhealthy and unviable.

To change behaviors and beliefs, you need to create a new, healthier pathway up that mountain. At first, it will feel difficult and unfamiliar. You may have to clumsily hack your way through dense brush. You may need to repeat the hike up and down the new path finding and re-finding your footing many times before you create a well-worn trail that feels natural for you to take. Meanwhile, the old path becomes so overgrown with thick brush from disuse that you don't even recognize it anymore. Now the new pathway has become your way of being.

This metaphor explains what doctors and scientists call neuroplasticity—the brain's ability to integrate new beliefs and behaviors. Repeating the rituals you're going to learn in Part Two will change your relationship with yourself, bringing you closer to your Original Blueprint® and liberating you from old, self-defeating habits. If you devote yourself to this work, you'll be living fearlessly, with great passion, openness, joy, and contentment.

There are no quick fixes on this journey. In the desire for instant gratification, people so often lose sight of the fact that anything worth having takes time and dedication to achieve. Your *devotion to a ritual creates a sacred pact* between you, your Original Blueprint®, and your Infinite Source. You must allow enough time for a ritual to become embodied. Trying to make drastic change in a short period of time won't work long term. It's more beneficial to devote yourself to **one** ritual that you think is the most important. Keep it simple, repeat it daily and you'll be successful. Whatever ritual you choose, be sure it engages the mind *and* body.

The exercises and rituals in this book are organized by skill level, so—depending on your level of personal experience in doing this kind of work—you may decide to jump around. You can skip exercises that don't resonate with you. That's perfectly fine. If something doesn't feel helpful or isn't aligned with your views, skip it.

Also, please feel free to modify a practice if another variation of it works better for you. Use the parts that work. You'll know what's working because your body will tell you that what you're experiencing is *different* and pleasant or neutral. Feeling *something different* means you're on a new mountain path, garnering new information about what your body needs. *"What's Different"* is a question we'll be referring to many times in Parts Two and Three and one you want to visit regularly throughout your journey. All answers are simply information for you to notice. We're simply looking for the awareness of *what's different.*

When you're doing an exercise or ritual, it's important to notice what's different in your body because the simple act of noticing the changes helps codify new neural pathways in your mind and new neurophysiology in your body. The act of noticing and then writing down your observations builds somatic awareness and intelligence. Increased somatic awareness strengthens the connection between your mind and body and is the key to embodiment. More awareness equals more regulation, more settling, and more presence in your daily life. Better and more creative decisions will arise from here.

One word of advice—lean into the areas and practices that feel *slightly* uncomfortable. These are probably the techniques you most need to learn because they will stretch you. So, if the thought of doing an exercise makes you feel a bit uncomfortable or nervous, don't immediately dismiss it. Try it out and see if it's something that might help. Stop if it's too much, but quite often these are exactly the exercises that will help you open to yourself more.

How do you know if an exercise is too much?

When the body releases what no longer serves us, you may feel tingling, warmth or coolness. Sometimes shaking can occur.

All of that is what we call *activation* and that's a good sign that you're on track! However, if the activation feels in any way overwhelming, **stop**. Go back to the exercises that didn't cause you to cross the overwhelm threshold. Everyone is different, *so take your time* moving through this work. Rushing the process or tolerating discomfort will slow your healing journey. More is not necessarily better. If the activation leaves your body by the next day and you find yourself feeling more in touch with your emotions and body awareness, those are indications that you're on track and can continue. Conversely, if in the following 48 hours, you are still experiencing discomfort, slow your journey down a bit. Take time for self care and return to an easier exercise or ritual at a later time.

Keep track of your experiences; specifically, take note of what's working best for you. At the end of the book, you'll reflect on what's most important for your long-term growth. Ask yourself: *What do I really care about? How do I plan to make it actionable?* If you can walk away with one ritual or commitment to carry forward, you'll be well on your way to being, as Gandhi once said, "the change you want to see in the world."

That ritual, commitment, intention, or purpose will be what you devote yourself to. I love the word devotion. It means having loyalty, faith, and an abiding love for something that's sacred. It means partnering under the guidance of something much bigger and more powerful than oneself. Your devotion to this work will pay off in extraordinary ways for you and others.

How will you know you're in communion with your Original Blueprint®? You'll be able to pressure-test traumatic memories, old fears, and wounds and find that they no longer have power over you. Your genuine nature will shine through—stronger than any fear you've felt in the past and you will feel more resilient. Embodying this truth will remind you that it's safe to be seen, to be known, and to be loved.

You'll no longer feel trapped or helpless in the face of life's challenges because balance, harmony and peace reside *within* you, always. Having full access to your mental and emotional reserves means that you won't dread the "negative" stuff in your life. Just keep your awareness on what feels different as you proceed, carefully noting the changes you're experiencing.

NOTE: If you have any physical limitations with any of the exercises or rituals (e.g., difficulty with nose breathing, sitting, or holding a certain posture), I celebrate you adjusting things to your comfort level. In fact, feeling comfortable in your body is very important; we don't want your body to feel forced into any of this work (there's enough of that in everyday life—sitting for hours, computer time, commuting in a car).

"The point is to be in a relationship with a higher power that can provide a container for your growth and healing. Embracing the infinite capacity of your Divine Source holds you in your suffering without judgment and provides the unconditional love you need to thrive."

WHAT'S CLEARER?

Has reading this overview clarified your understanding of the difference between exercises and rituals, and why developing healthy rituals is crucial to changing old patterns? Has it shed any light on why past "self-improvement" efforts may not have succeeded? What do you feel encouraged to do differently now?

Write your thoughts in your *Companion Workbook* or in your personal journal.

"

As human beings, our greatness lies not so much in being able to remake the world—that is a myth of the atomic age—as in being able to remake ourselves.

- Mahatma Gandhi

CHAPTER FIVE

Leaning on Your Village Matters

It's impossible for healing to happen in isolation. As we're able to now recognize, the desire for connection with others supports our personal growth ten-fold. We are souls who have come into bodies to give us the experience of *separateness*.

This loss of *oneness* for our souls only happens when the soul inhabits a body—it's our unique moment to know what it means to be human—to be separated. Separation is humankind's greatest assignment. It challenges us to overcome our fear of differences (us versus them) and be a full participant in our global village in positive ways. You cannot fully be in your Original Blueprint® without being a connected, compassionate, engaged human being who is actively—and beneficially—supporting our global village. In so doing, you are already purposeful.

There are four aspects that shape and condition human beings and create the internal ecosystem in which our core beliefs about the world form. These four aspects—*beliefs, community, lineage, and rituals*—establish the foundation of one's social-emotional worldview. In Part One of this book, we covered each of these aspects and explored why they're important parts of the journey back to your Original Blueprint®. Here in Chapter Five, you will explore how to use each aspect to move from where you are to where you want to be.

"The loss of oneness the soul experiences by inhabiting a body is unique to being human. It challenges you to learn how to overcome your perception of separateness while you're here. You do that by overcoming your fear of differences (us versus them) and by being a full participant in our global village in beneficial ways."

Exploring your perspectives will lay the groundwork for a deeper understanding of yourself, your desires, and your place in the world. Delving into these facets of your village also helps you understand how the *communal* intersects with the *individual,* and how the *personal* becomes a manifestation of the *universal.* Most importantly, making the effort to lay a durable foundation will allow the work that comes after this to be meaningful, rich, and transformative.

Support Systems

As you go through these exercises about your support systems here in Chapter Five, answer these questions as truthfully as you can. Write your answers in a personal journal or ideally, in *The Paper Tiger Syndrome Companion Workbook* (visit IrisInstitute.com to download the workbook), which is designed specifically to guide you along this journey. The *Companion Workbook* has an expanded version of the Parts Two and Three rituals and exercises laid out in an easy, step-by-step format. Make the effort to use your *Companion Workbook* or your personal journal to faithfully record the thoughts, feelings, and insights that arise as a result of your work.

Take as much time as you need to record the answers to each question, as well as all the questions and exercises that are to come. And don't settle for surface or automatic answers; the more detailed your inventory, the more benefit you'll get from it. This is where we get to apply what you've learned so far, so don't short-change yourself!

Personal Beliefs

Whether or not you consider yourself to be a member of a religion, everyone has belief systems about how they imagine the world works. Your belief systems are one of the foundational pillars upon which you build your life. And since all aspects of life are interconnected, you can't separate your belief systems from the primary morals and values of the community into which you were born. This is true whether you've embraced the beliefs of your village or rebelled against them. Either way, it's necessary to explore in greater depth your beliefs and how they've shaped you.

Still, if you find any of the exercises unhelpful or not relevant to you, remember that it's all right to skip them. For example, the idea that one "should" have a religious or spiritual practice offends some people. If this describes you, then simply skip the questions that pertain to religion or spirituality. However, I do advise being open to an expanded idea of what spirituality means to you. Make it yours.

I often say that nature or the universe are examples of infinite capacity that exist all around us. If you don't believe in a God (or Gods), you may find it helpful to write about nature, the universe or some other representation of an Infinite Source that resonates with you. Ask yourself, *in what ways does this (or could this) relationship with something infinite support me?*

Why does it matter if you connect with something that you believe has infinite capacity? As I've stated before, human beings aren't naturally designed to be alone. We're here to help each other. We're pack animals that do better when we work together and support each other. Support is one of the most important aspects of community. Too much isolation damages the spirit. But having the courage to lean on the people who care about you is what community is all about. The same principle holds true for your relationship with your Infinite Source—stay in relationship with it and you'll find it will fortify you for a lifetime.

From the time I was very young, I felt a sense that there was something bigger than me out there. There was more to life than just what I could see on this earth. My family and village never dictated that I follow one strict, religious path. My spiritual range was eclectic. My mother raised me in the Jewish faith. But my father wasn't Jewish; he was a secular Christian, so this exposed me and my sister to Christianity, too.

As an adult, I've exposed myself to experiences with Islam, Buddhism and Sufism. I've attended just about every religious service out there. Later, I found comfort and belonging in support groups and 12-step programs for people whose family members were addicts. All these experiences have shaped my own unique set of beliefs.

As I grew older, I found that I also gained peace and connectedness from being in nature. My mother took my sister and me out into nature just about every weekend during our teen years. We would hike up in the mountains all the time and camp in the forests. We were blessed to be born into a family that respected and nurtured our desire for a deep connection to (what I call) the Divine—something that had an infinite capacity to hold me through life.

I felt supported by all of it. My household didn't assign labels, judgments, or assumptions about organized religion. I didn't grow up in a community that believed in proselytizing. In fact, because of the Jewish people's history of forced conversions, proselytizing is antithetical to the religion. I learned that beliefs are sacred, individual, and personal. (I am sharing my own views on beliefs with you because I want you to know that I am in no way attempting to sway your beliefs—they are a very personal choice.)

This ethos shaped who I am today. I have a daily gratitude practice. Each night, I engage in this practice of appreciation, which keeps me grounded and connected to my Infinite Source. Like any relationship, I've cultivated and nurtured the unique connection that I have now with my Divine Source, which has helped me get through everything big and small and to delight in every moment of my life, whether I've felt afraid or fully present.

Over the years, I have deepened this relationship so much that the changing circumstances of life no longer hold much fear for me; I trust that whatever happens in the world, I'll be fine. Even when things are completely out of my control, the outcome isn't so important to me anymore. I am at peace. I am content inside and savor every moment like a warm cup of yummy tea. I am grateful for what I have for as long as I have it. Spirituality for me has been my saving grace.

Sometimes people wrestle with spirituality. They may be going through a dark night of the soul. Or maybe don't really have faith in a higher power. Sometimes people grow up in proselytizing communities where they're taught to believe that "it's our way or you're doomed." In those instances, the idea of believing in something larger than yourself can become scary or unpalatable rather than supportive. But, in this book, we're talking about how to overcome fear. And any religion that attempts to keep you in fear is not in service of a higher, infinite power. Fear is a cheap marketing tool to keep you in line. Fear is *not* the way any Infinite Source wants us to feel. We're here to discover love for all that is in us and around us.

A spiritual practice steeped in *your* truth will impart an abiding faith, along with the understanding that an infinite capacity is holding you all the time. Your focus is simply to cultivate and deepen a relationship with that higher being, however you wish to define it. For our work, it doesn't matter what you call it. If you call it nature, great. If you call it science or the Universe, great. If it's God, great. This isn't the place to get caught up in the "rights" and "wrongs" of religiosity.

The important thing to remember is that we're not alone. We're never alone. Any thought to the contrary is an illusion. Look no further than the gravity holding you right now to know that you are being held by something much bigger than you. The more that you cultivate a relationship with something outside of yourself, something that's bigger, grander and has the capacity to hold you, the more you're going to feel a sense of safety and contentment. You'll feel more open and spacious. Your mind expands, while simultaneously being calm and settled. That's what we're talking about—living with the feeling that, *No matter what, I am loved. I am enough. I am fearless!*

Beginning Level Exercise: Belief Systems

In this exercise, I invite you to write about your relationship with something in your life that has infinite capacity—however you define that (nature, higher power, science, Universe, Infinite One, Creator, God, Divine, Jesus, Vishnu, Shiva, Source, Buddha, Allah, Adonai, Yahweh, etc.). All relationships desire to be tended to regularly. Your relationship with your Source is no different.

Use the *Companion Workbook* or your journal to answer these questions:

- What ways does this/these relationship(s) support you?
- How do you regularly stay connected to this relationship?
- How do you lean on this relationship when things are challenging?
- How do you show appreciation for this relationship when you are flourishing?
- Is there anything you would like to do differently to cultivate more from this relationship?

Beginning Level Exercise: Community

The quality of your connections is far more important than the quantity. You can have a million followers on social media and feel completely isolated. So, if you have a small community or a small group of people who you feel are truly supportive in your life, great! If you have at least one other person you feel intimately connected to, you face much less risk of experiencing the negative health effects of isolation. That one person could be your therapist. It may be your doctor. It can be a co-worker or a neighbor. It can also be a pet. It can be anybody who you feel is truly there for you, who you can call on when you need someone. Think about who this is for you.

Take an inventory—with as much specificity as possible—of who already supports you.

In your *Companion Workbook* or journal, ask yourself:

- Who are your sources of inspiration? Reflect on any family members, surrogate family, friends, leaders (alive or not) and groups that you look to for inspiration and/or support.

- Why is this person (or persons) so important to you?
- What is it like to feel fully seen, acknowledged, and accepted for who you are?
- What is it like to be that person for someone else?
- Again, if you can't think of anyone specific that you feel intimately connected to, ask yourself who you might like to invite into your inner circle. Do you feel comfortable (or at least willing) to initiate a deeper connection with that person?

Continue the list you've already begun to assemble by naming those people in your life who are present (or here in spirit) who support you completely.

In your *Companion Workbook* or journal answer the following questions:

- Write a few sentences or a paragraph detailing what you appreciate about them.
- Why are you most grateful for them?
- In what ways do you express your gratitude for their support?
- Have you told them lately how important they are to you?

Remember, these people can be anyone in your life whose presence provides you with strength and comfort (family, ancestors, friends, coworkers, neighbors, pets, social groups, support groups, exercise groups). And if you can't think of someone you feel close and connected to, write about ways that you can work on establishing one or two new, supportive relationships in your life.

Intermediate Level Exercise: Lineage

When talking about lineage and community, it's important to look at this line of inquiry from multiple vantage points. It's not straightforward. First, think about friends, family, community members, ancestors, co-workers, and the like.

In your *Companion Workbook* or journal, ask yourself:

- Write a list of people who are part of your family line, as far back as you can remember, particularly the people who've had a direct impact on your life.
- Add to that list the people from your community who you interact with on a regular or semi-regular basis. Who are the people you know and love, but with whom you don't speak very often? There may be people on the list with whom you want to form a stronger connection. Put a mark next to those names. Write out some ideas for deepening those connections.

For some people, making a list like this can be difficult. Issues such as estrangement or abandonment are more common in families than people realize. Or a person may be adopted and have little or no information about their biological family; in this case, list your chosen family. And, for others, communities of people have lost their cultural origins altogether.

For example, there are millions of people of color in the United States whose ancestors were enslaved; there are indigenous people across the globe who've lost their traditions after centuries of destruction and annihilation. They live with the reality that they may never know all the names of their direct ancestors.

The examples of marginalized people are endless. For many they still can feel intergenerational pain on a deeply personal level. These are conundrums that regularly arise when we talk about the importance of lineage. So, it's important to be sensitive to the fact some of us don't know basic information about our ancestral line.

If any of these or other examples apply to you or someone you love, I want to further clarify what I mean when I refer to the notion of lineage. In these instances, I have people begin this exercise by invoking their lineage as *people, those who are named and unnamed, known and unknown, who are part of your ancestral line. Even when you cannot specifically identify them, they are still part of you. They are in your DNA. They're in every cellular structure of your body. You are the result of the love of thousands of people who've walked this earth before you.*

Their power, wisdom, intelligence, strength, and beauty live inside you, whether you've experienced a personal connection to them or not. When you look in the mirror and you see your stunning face looking back at you, that's your lineage. You are, in fact, millions of years old! Lineage can be more about how you feel than what you know. This is the place to begin exploring all of that.

In your *Companion Workbook* or journal, ask yourself:

- What aspects of your lineage delight you and give you a sense of pride?
- What do you know about the people who came before you?
- What things have left you wondering, perhaps for many years?
- What do you already embody from your lineage?

Are you powerful? Are you kind? Are you confident? Are you beautiful? Here's a chance to explore how all of that history gets expressed every day, through you and around you.

In your *Companion Workbook* or journal, ask yourself:

- What parts of your lineage are most alive in you and around you in your everyday life?

- Who are the people in your community who you trust the most?
- Who's the honest person in your life who gives you genuine feedback?
- Who do you trust to give you insight when you feel afraid or confused?
- Who will listen to you talk about your revelations and stumbling blocks?
- Who do you lean on, who supports you and has your back no matter what troubles you face? Is it one person or do you have more than one?
- If you can't think of specific individuals in your life who serve these functions, list some people that you'd like to get closer to. With whom would you like to develop a deeper bond? How could you initiate that connection?

Let's now look at the things that may be frightening or scary about your lineage. I invite you to be radically honest with yourself about the parts of your lineage that maybe aren't so flattering. Every lineage has a history of atrocious actions and it's important to acknowledge and forgive ourselves—*and each other*—for it. Shame holds no place in our Original Blueprint®. We are working to create a holistic and realistic view of who we are—not a fantastical version of ourselves that denies the ugliness and hardship that sometimes happens in life.

In your *Companion Workbook* or journal, ask yourself:

- What parts of my family's lineage have I tried to deny or overlook?
- What aspects of my lineage are painful or evoke shame?
- Are there things about my family (or specific people in the family) that I feel afraid to face?

111

- Now that I've looked at it, how can I take action in the world to pay it forward in some way—and release the fear, shame, denial and pain or the bypassing that I often do in an attempt to rid myself of that pain? (If this is a big one for you, flag this one so you can continue to work on it in Chapter Nine, when you explore your legacy).

Before you continue, check in with yourself and see if there are any feelings of overwhelm in your body. If you notice a tightness in your chest, shallower breathing, or some agitation, do this exercise before proceeding:

Stand up, bend your head and torso forward so that the upper half of your body is at a 90 degree angle. Let your arms and shoulders go fully limp. Now, shake the upper half of your body like a ragdoll, moving down toward your feet and back up to a standing posture. Repeat this 3-5 times. Then come back to a resting state. I call this the *Ragdoll* and it's how all animals shake off activation after a traumatic encounter. This ritual is one of my personal favorites to release stress or overwhelm. See if you can notice anything different in your body, then continue.

Intermediate Level Exercise: Existing Rituals

A ritual is anything that you can repeat, that engages all of you and feeds your soul. Rituals help keep you grounded in a commitment to something larger than yourself. Prayer, meditation, exercise, cooking, gardening, drawing, painting, knitting, playing an instrument—anything that helps fortify your mind and body you can use as a ritual for healing and self-regulation. Having previously covered the crucial nature of rituals, it's fair to say that your ability to sustain a healthy ritual will determine the level of success you have in this work. Once you start (or continue) this long love affair with something you fully devote yourself to, it's hard to imagine life without it.

Rituals are about cultivating more ways to *regularly* connect to something outside of yourself, too. Devotion to a ritual makes people more self-reflective and embodied. The more you're devoted to one ritual, the more you get good at it, the more that it becomes your new way. That's why we don't want to take on more than a couple of new rituals at one time. When your focus is split in too many directions, you can't get the full benefit of any one thing.

- List the rituals you have in place that sustain you. How often do you repeat your rituals? What do the rituals mean to you (prayer, meditation, restorative yoga, hiking, walking, cooking, gardening, drawing, painting, knitting, playing an instrument, etc.). Remember that rituals are practices that you need to repeat to embody them.

If you've seen the documentary film, *Jiro Dreams of Sushi*, you know that the film tells an inspiring story of revered sushi chef Jiro Ono who strives for perfection is his work while his eldest son fiercely attempts to live up to his father's legacy. Japan's centuries-old tradition of ritual and the repetition of practice plays out in the backdrop of this film. To become really good at something, we must devote ourselves—like Jiro's love of sushi—to being in a long apprenticeship and love affair with it.

Commitment to Practice

Jean-Paul Sartre once wrote, "Commitment is an act, not a word." When you commit to something, the act of fulfilling that commitment requires being true to yourself, even in the face of great adversity. It requires focused intention and a clear vision for what you want to achieve or experience. Commitment requires that you clearly define what is most important to you and then find the motivation to stay the course until you attain it (which may be brief or for a lifetime and then some!).

Looking back at the aspects of your village that we've examined in this chapter, ask yourself and write down in your *Companion Workbook* or journal:

- Is there someone or something you want to commit (or re-commit) yourself to?

Of course, you don't have to if it doesn't feel relevant at this moment. But this is a chance to reflect on whether you think there's a way to go deeper into your healing work. Pay attention to your degree of ambition. If you've got enough right now, you don't need to commit to something else. Continue with what you have. It's important that you're successful with whatever you're doing, rather than getting disappointed because you've taken on too much. The key to success is to keep it simple. Make sure that whatever you choose for your commitment, it engages all of you—mind, spirit, and body.

In your *Companion Workbook* or journal:

- Name one relationship and/or ritual you'd like to start this year and your commitment (or re-commitment) to deepen it.

- Complete this sentence:

  I commit to [relationship or ritual] that I will [action and frequency] so that [outcome you're seeking].

  Here's an example:
  I commit to [my wife] that I will [organize date night] [every

week] so that [we feel more connected to each other].

Exactly how do you intend to hold yourself accountable and who can support you with honoring your commitment?

You can find this Commitment to Practice Worksheet and other worksheets, links to video and audio demos, and other helpful materials at IrisInstitute.com.

REFLECTIONS

WHAT'S CLEARER?

After reading this chapter, what's clearer to you that you want to be sure and remember? Write your thoughts down in the *Companion Workbook* or in your personal journal.

Get the Companion Workbook @ IrisInstitute.com

> *Awareness is like the sun. When it shines on things, they are transformed.*
>
> - Eckhart Tolle

CHAPTER SIX

When Mind Meets Body and Falls in Love

My wish for you is that if nothing else arises from reading this book, you will gain a deeper sense of yourself just from this chapter alone. If that happens, then I believe you will have the essential support you need to be far more present in your life, less fear-driven and much more content in yourself than before you began this journey with me. *Body awareness—specifically the ritual of interoception—is the key to self-regulation.*

Where do you notice the sensation of hunger? What internal sensations tell you when you're tired and need sleep? Reflect on the last time you felt joyful or grateful. Where, exactly, did the sensation of these emotions reside in your body? What about anxiety, anger, or grief? Where do these reside in you?

Emotions are felt in the body. We can *think* about an emotion but that's quite different than *feeling the sensation* of the emotion. As we've discussed, somatic awareness is the ability to tune into our bodies at any given time and recognize what's going on inside ourselves. It's the recognition that our minds and bodies must live as one functioning unit, if we want to experience a healthy, well-rounded life. That symbiotic relationship is the most elemental building block of embodiment and the Original Blueprint®.

Human beings instinctively have this connection between mind and body, but we pay such little attention to it in our modern world that we largely have lost the profound meaning of that connection, especially in the West. And because the sensation of our emotions resides in the body, having a well-developed sense of body awareness increases our emotional intelligence, too. Emotional intelligence is defined as "the ability to identify and name one's own emotions; the ability to harness those emotions and apply them to tasks such as thinking and problem solving; and the ability to manage emotions, which includes both regulating one's own emotions when necessary and helping others do the same."

It's time to begin simple rituals that will show you *how* to cultivate and maintain self-regulation and all the benefits that come with it. So, whether you get it right away or spend months developing these skills, it's worth taking the time to understand and, it is my hope for you, to master the techniques outlined here. When you do, you'll have the ability to live more fearlessly and with greater presence with what is...regardless of the circumstances.

Mind-Body Match Up

The rituals that you will learn in this chapter will teach you to identify and release activation (again, activation is when you experience those heightened physical sensations that keep you on high alert). These rituals will allow you more access to regulate your nervous system and manage your emotions. As you know, when people lack strong body awareness and a regulated nervous system, they can develop maladaptive coping mechanisms to deal with the painful ups and downs of life (e.g., self-medication to numb, escape, deny). But well-developed, body-oriented awareness permits us to notice stress, anxiety, and tension much faster and deal with the root causes, rather than internalizing the distressing symptoms.

The first step is to be able to ground yourself with the world around you. That means you have somatic awareness of the immediate contact the body has with the outside world. Another word for this is *proprioception*. Proprioception is knowing instinctively where a light switch is in a darkened room or type on a keyboard without looking at every key. Human beings also have vestibular senses—mechanisms in our inner ear—which control balance and head movement. You can use all your senses to become keen observers of the world around you and your place in it.

Beginning Level Ritual: Proprioception Warmup

Please be sure that you're seated in a comfortable position now (adjust if you need to). If you can, close your eyes, and breathe naturally (if closing your eyes causes them to flutter, open them slightly and cast your gaze downward). See if you can notice contact between your body and the support (chair or floor) behind you and beneath you. Locate your feet and feel the contact with what's beneath them (socks, soles of the shoes, layers of material, all the way down to the earth's surface). Now see if you can notice the gravitational pull between your body and the earth. What's it like for you to notice any or all this support around you? Now, jot down your experience here or make a mental note of what it's like to notice your surroundings:

- What's different for you now, if anything, than what you experienced before this practice? Do you find yourself calmer or more settled? Sometimes simply noticing gravity's pull to keep us supported can help us settle.

Beginning Level Ritual: Grounding

Grounding is a ritual that connects your spiritual and physical self to the earth. It will steady you and create energetic balance, which allows you to connect more authentically with the mind and body.

Try it. Begin by relaxing the places in your body that hold tension—check your shoulders and slowly roll them. Check your neck and slowly roll it. Check your jaw by stretching your mouth wide open, then relaxing the jaw back into itself with the top and bottom teeth slightly separated. With your mouth more relaxed, soften your tongue and rest it on the lower palette of your mouth. These adjustments will put you more in touch with your body for the grounding work (and all the other rituals and exercises you'll be learning).

Bring your attention to your breathing and take a long, slow, deep inhalation through your nose. Hold it for three seconds, or a little longer if you can do so with ease. Then exhale a nice, long exhalation through your mouth. Repeat this *very slowly*. Nice, long, deep—but effortless—breath...in through the nose, out through the mouth. Repeat this practice five times. This ritual can be done throughout your day to remain present in your body. You can use this ritual as your transition practice—between meetings, before and after work, and so on.

Grounding is a basic—but essential—practice to help you deepen your body awareness and learn more about how to self-regulate. If you find that you don't notice any sensation below your neck when you do this ritual, I recommend staying with grounding by pausing here and practicing this exercise until you notice a sensation (heartbeat, temperatures in your chest, rise and fall of the chest during breathing, sit bones supporting you, feet making contact with the ground, etc.).

WHAT'S DIFFERENT?

Beginning/Intermediate Level Somatic Dimensions
Noticing Inner Experience

Refer to the examples in Figure 6 (below) to describe your inner experience (aka, interoception) or add your own:

Anxious	Grounded	Relaxed
Breathy	Heart Beating	Settled
Buzzy	Warmer	Slower
Calmer	Overwhelmed	Stressed
Cooler	Pulsing	Tingling

Fig. 6

Use the *Companion Workbook* or journal to answer these questions:

Before this ritual, my body's experience was...
After this ritual, my body is more/less...

Beginning Level Ritual: Engaging the Five Senses

The next ritual serves as a bridge between the outside world (proprioception) and the internal world (interoception). Please note that we'll get into more deeply defining and working with interoception after this transition exercise but for now, know that interoception is awareness of your inner experience. Each ritual below engages one of your five senses. Slowly practice each one and notice the connection between the outer world of the sense you're in and how it connects you inside:

- Connect with *smell* by using aromatherapy, incense, fruit, fresh air, etc.
- Connect with *touch* by moving the palms of your hands down your legs, then back up again.
- Connect with *sound* through calming music, chimes, etc.
- Connect with *sight* by appreciating beauty in the world.
- Connect with *taste* by slowly eating something delicious.

Slowly repeat each of these rituals for three minutes until all your senses are available to you.

REFLECTIONS
COMPANION WORKBOOK/JOURNAL

WHAT'S DIFFERENT?

Beginning/Intermediate Level Somatic Dimensions
Noticing Inner Experience

Refer to the examples in Figure 7 (below) to describe your inner experience (aka, interoception) or add your own:

Anxious	Grounded	Relaxed
Breathy	Heart Beating	Settled
Buzzy	Warmer	Slower
Calmer	Overwhelmed	Stressed
Cooler	Pulsing	Tingling

Fig. 7

Use the *Companion Workbook* or journal to answer these questions:

Before this ritual, my body's experience was...
After this ritual, my body is more/less...

Understanding the Most Essential Ritual: Interoception

The most *essential work* you'll learn in this book is embodying the concept of *interoception*. Interoception is the mind's ability to notice what's happening *inside* the body. This engages your brain's medial prefrontal cortex (known as the "third eye" in eastern philosophy)—the observing part of our brain. Over time, rituals that support interoception will dissipate stress and anxiety, so long as our attention is down in our body (and not in our thoughts). This takes repetition and practice.

In this chapter, you'll learn to first notice sensation in your body and then expand into other dimensions of awareness and imagination (e.g., images, colors, shapes, emotions, and varying weights/densities). As I (and others) like to define it: **interoception is the *mind falling in love* with the body.** Moreover, I believe that once you are highly proficient at it, *interoception offers you a deeper connection with your soul and the relationship you have with your Infinite Source.* When the two are in communion, their relationship is essential to feeling safe and living fearlessly. *If you go no further in this book than mastering interoception, you will have the essential ritual you need to be far more present in your life!*

Our modern world has separated mind and body for so long that it's difficult for most people to even imagine the experience of their union. Interoception work is uncommon. Our culture mostly rewards our intellect. Even in mindfulness, the emphasis is often on releasing or observing our thoughts to stay grounded in the present moment. *What we're talking about with interoception is a quieting of the constant impulses of the mind and being in the silence of your soul, which resides in your body.*

Being masterful with interoception means we also learn to engage with the world around us more powerfully. For example, compelling and embodied speakers learn to speak from their bellies as opposed to their minds.

"Interoception is the mind falling in love with the body... it offers you a deeper connection with your soul and the sacred relationship you have with your Infinite Source...This relationship is essential to feeling safe and living fiercely.... If you go no further in this book than mastering interoception, you will have the essential ritual you need to be fully present in your life."

As we touched on in Chapter Two, when the nervous system is dysregulated (feeling unsafe), it goes into either hyper- or hypo-activation. Like the gas and breaks on a car, hyperactivation is the raising of your sympathetic charge beyond your optimal range—anxiety and other stress-related conditions happen here. We're pressing too hard on the gas pedal. Conversely, hypoactivation is related more to low energy, shutdown, or depression. We've hit the brakes instead of easing into a slowdown. That's when the crash-and-burn happens. Your internal engine has "run out of steam."

Everyone has a *Window of Resilience*, which is his unique, optimal range of capacity to navigate thoughts and emotions without overwhelm or shutdown. When you're in this window, you have enough resilience to dissolve or dilute the unpleasant aspects of life, such as stress and anxiety, which can bring you closer to the edges of your window of resilience. When you're in your resilience window, you're also deepening your ability to be with life's pleasant aspects—presence, joy, gratitude, intimacy, love and more. This is the sweet spot where there's a balance between sympathetic (your giddy-up-and-go) and parasympathetic (your rest and digest).

After mastering interoception, not only will you be able to recognize when you're nearing the edges of your window, you'll also have the tools you need to bring yourself back into resilience (Figure 8).

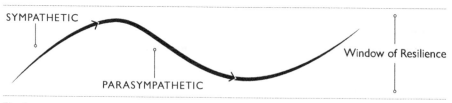

SYMPATHETIC

Window of Resilience

PARASYMPATHETIC

Fig. 8

WINDOW OF RESILIENCE
Feelings and reactions are viable; we can think and feel simultaneously; our reactions adapt to fit the situation.

Under stress, the nervous system can falsely perceive threat and go into a survival reaction, which pushes you far outside your window of resilience (Figure 9). Of course, if it's a real threat, the nervous system will automatically—and wisely—take over to protect you.

SIGNS OF CHRONIC HYPERACTIVATION
Emotional overwhelm, panic, impulsivity, hypervigilance, defensiveness, feeling unsafe, reactive, angry, racing thoughts.

Fig. 9

SIGNS OF CHRONIC HYPOACTIVATION
Numb, "dead," passive, no feelings, no energy, can't think, disconnected, shut down, "not there," ashamed, can't say "no".

Look closely at your nervous system's tendency. Do you default more often to hyperactivation or hypoactivation? Or do you go in between the two and then crash-and-burn? Do you work long hours during the week, then crash and sleep in late on the weekends?

We can learn to stay within our window of resilience, as best as we can. When actual or perceived danger is present the nervous system takes over in a split second, choosing our best survival strategy for us (fight, flight, or freeze). Of course, our bodies' protection system is never going to respond with complete accuracy. There will still be times in the future when your nervous system spikes outside your window when it shouldn't, when it responds to a perceived threat instead of real one. But by and large, we can mostly learn how to be in our window of resilience, notice when we're edging out, and apply the tools in this chapter to get back inside the window.

You may be asking, *What can I pay attention to so that I recognize the edges of my window of resilience?* If you begin to experience any of the common responses outlined in Figure 10 and you are just at the initial stage of feeling low levels of discomfort or unpleasantness, you want to use the essential tools outlined later in this chapter to move yourself back into the window of resilience.

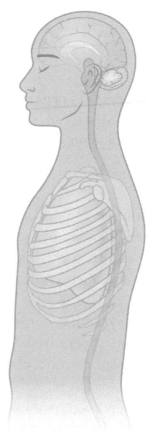

Sympathetic
Rapid speech
Increased movement
Dilated pupils
Watery eyes
Dry mouth
Perspiration
Increased heart rate
Increased adrenaline
Shallow breathing
Decreased digestion
Relaxed bladder

Parasympathetic
Stimulated digestion
Pupil constriction
Dry eyes
Increased salivation
Slower heart rate
Slower, deeper breathing
Peristalsis
Contracted bladder

Fig. 10

Repetition of an interoception ritual will put you back inside your resilience window where you'll be in touch with your body again, primarily through sensation that mostly happens in your chest and belly. Over time, you'll stay more within your window and experience greater capacity and resilience to embrace anything that comes your way.

As you try these rituals, write about your experiences and see if you can make your answers as descriptive as possible. What do you notice before the ritual? More anxiety, tension, or stress? Afterwards, is your body more settled, calm, or spacious? Where, specifically, do you notice these differences in your body? As with all the rituals and exercises you'll be doing, GO VERY SLOWLY so that the changes you're seeking have time to integrate. Remember: This isn't a race to the finish line; you don't want to skip to the next ritual without receiving the benefits of the one you're in.

Intermediate Level Ritual: Interoception Warmup

Focus on the first and most essential dimension of interoception—sensation (we will explore the other dimensions to deepen your somatic awareness soon).

Run in place for 60 seconds or if you can't run in place, do jumping jacks, sit in a chair and make a bicycling motion or raise your legs up-and-down or whatever adaption works for you to increase your heart rate. After 60 seconds, take your pulse on your wrist or neck or put your hand on your heart. Notice the increased heart/pulse rate from running in place—that is your nervous system in the giddy-up-and-go (sympathetic). Now notice how the heart rate/pulse begins to decrease over time—that is your nervous system moving into the rest and digest (parasympathetic).

Noticing these dimensions is the start of body awareness (interoception). Continue with this ritual for three minutes daily until you notice at least one of these dimensions. Sometimes we need more time with the essentials of interoception. If this applies to you, repeat this ritual until you feel masterful with it. If it isn't available to you, that's okay. Stay with this ritual until your awareness changes. Keep answering the following questions as your awareness builds:

REFLECTIONS
COMPANION WORKBOOK/JOURNAL

WHAT'S DIFFERENT?

Beginning/Intermediate Level Somatic Dimensions
Noticing Inner Experience

Use the examples in Figure 11 (below) to describe your inner experience (aka, interoception) or add your own:

Anxious	Grounded	Relaxed
Breathy	Heart Beating	Settled
Buzzy	Warmer	Slower
Calmer	Overwhelmed	Stressed
Cooler	Pulsing	Tingling

Fig. 11

Use the *Companion Workbook* or journal to answer these questions:

Before this ritual, my body's experience was...
After this ritual, my body is more/less...

The key to presence is sensation. Being "present" is a term that we have made more complicated than it actually is: *If you can notice a sensation of any dimension (like a feeling, color, shape, image, temperature, weight, movement) somewhere in your body, you're present. It's that simple. **And interoception is the ritual that gets you to presence.***

For example, noticing the temperature of your breath entering your nose, mouth, or throat—that's presence. Or feeling your heart rate—that's presence. Or the rise and fall of your chest, lungs expanding and contracting with each inhale and exhale of your breath. That's presence. Feeling peristalsis—the movement of food through the digestive track—is presence. And so on. Presence creates the conditions to inhabit a regulated nervous system, which is the most essential component to accessing your Original Blueprint®. Interoception is how you become embodied in your life, regulated in your body, and how you learn to live confidently and fearlessly.

Intermediate Level Ritual: Interoception Using Mindful Breathwork

One of the simplest and most essential forms of interoception comes to us through mindful breathing. The emotional and physical benefits of a breathwork ritual are widely known. The practice of mindful breathing gets credit for everything from stress relief, lowering anxiety and reducing blood pressure to enhancing spiritual experiences. Some say mindful breathwork is the key to slowing down cognitive decline and to keeping the brain and body healthy and the spirit young.

NOTE: If you have a physical limitation (e.g., difficulty with nose breathing) that requires you to adjust the following ritual, it's okay to adjust to your comfort level.

Before you begin, read these instructions fully:

Step 1 Place one hand on your heart space—right in the center of your chest—and the other on your belly. This contact will help anchor your awareness in the body. As you breathe, begin to pay attention to what you notice inside, right underneath your hands.

Step 2 Now *slowly* take a long, effortless in-breath through your nose, followed by a long, slow out-breath through your mouth. Support the settling in your body by putting space between the top and bottom teeth and softening your tongue to rest on the lower palette of your mouth (doing the opposite increases anxiety and stress). Make this dance between the in-breath and out-breath effortless—just the right amount of inhaling so that you begin to slowly go deeper into your long out-breaths and notice more spaciousness inside.

Repeat this ritual for three minutes. Answer the "What's Different" questions on the following page.

REFLECTIONS
COMPANION WORKBOOK/JOURNAL

WHAT'S DIFFERENT?

Refer to the examples in Figure 12 (below) to describe your inner experience (aka, interoception) or add your own:

Beginning/Intermediate Level Somatic Dimensions
Noticing Inner Experience

Anxious	Grounded	Relaxed
Breathy	Heart Beating	Settled
Buzzy	Warmer	Slower
Calmer	Overwhelmed	Stressed
Cooler	Pulsing	Tingling

Fig. 12

Use the *Companion Workbook* or journal to answer these questions:

Before this ritual, my body's experience was...
After this ritual, my body is more/less...
See if you can notice *where* in the body you feel different...

Advanced Level Ritual: Interoception—Beyond Sensation

Sensation is the first of five dimensions of body awareness. You can build on the interoception ritual by incorporating awareness of the four other dimensions: image, actions/behavior, emotions/affect and meaning.

In the quest to liberate myself and my clients from fear and chronic stress, there are few therapeutic modalities I've found as powerful as Somatic Experiencing®, the pioneering work of Dr. Peter Levine. Dr. Levine identified five dimensions of awareness—sensation, image, behavior, affect and meaning, adapted, and simplified here from his original work noted in his book, *In an Unspoken Voice*:

1. **Sensation:** The essential awareness of internal sensations, including pulse, colors, varying weights and temperatures. For example:

- *I notice the temperature of my breath coming into my nostrils or throat.*
- *I notice a warm, gooey red blob in my heart space.*
- *I notice the pull of gravity in my sit bones and thighs.*
- *I notice my heart beating in my chest.*
- *I can feel lunch moving through my belly (peristalsis)!*

2. **Image:** Using what you already know from your senses (sight, sound, smell, touch, taste) see if you can access the image of something pleasant arising from within you. This is a tricky one to explain (easier to experience) but here are a few examples:

- *(Sight) I can feel the lower half of my body settling when I imagine seeing my dog napping.*
- *(Sound) I notice a settling inside my chest when I imagine the sound of a bird chirping.*

- *(Smell) I feel more calm in my belly when I imagine the smell of a pine forest.*
- *(Touch) I notice my back relaxing when I imagine being held by a warm blanket.*
- *(Taste) I notice laughter arising from my belly when I imagine the sweet taste of my mother's blueberry pie.*

3. **Behavior:** Any observable changes, including skin temperature, breath rate, pace of speech or actual movements like rocking, reaching, foot-tapping, yawning, and so on.

- *I notice the movement of my calves, swinging up and back, just like when I was a kid!*
- *I notice my shoulders shrugging and shaking off the experience.*
- *I notice that I'm yawning in this moment.*

4. **Affect:** Emotions and emotional experiences becoming more available, such as calm, settled, peaceful, restful, spacious, open and irritability, agitation, anger.

- *I am noticing contentment and gratitude in my heart space.*
- *I feel open and spacious inside, right in my chest and belly.*
- *I am noticing anger in my gut and it's energizing!*

5. **Meaning:** Verbal narrative of self, other or an event as well as any form of abstracted relationship.

- *I'm noticing this feeling of being safe means I can be more expressive, more alive, or more connected to others.*
- *I'm noticing I'm much calmer after recognizing that I'm not responsible for other people's reactions.*
- *I'm noticing that when I let go of trying to control my partner, I can relax and be vulnerable with her.*

Begin your ritual of interoception with a warmup. Then move into the interoception ritual using mindful breathwork. Over time, as you become more comfortable with the ritual, see if you can be more descriptive of your internal experience by noticing some of the other dimensions of body awareness beyond the sensation of your breath. For the sake of ease, I've repeated the mindfulness ritual here:

Interoception Using Mindful Breathwork

Place one hand on your heart space and the other on your belly. This contact will help anchor your awareness in the body. As you breathe, begin to pay attention to what you notice inside, right underneath your hands.

Now *slowly* begin taking a long, effortless in-breath through your nose, followed by a long, slow out-breath through your mouth. Support the settling in your body by putting space between the top and bottom teeth and softening your tongue to rest on the lower palette of your mouth (doing the opposite increases anxiety and stress). Make this dance between the in-breath and out-breath effortless—just the right amount of inhaling so that you begin to slowly go deeper into your long out-breaths and notice more spaciousness inside.

Stay with this ritual for at least three minutes.

In addition to sensation, what other dimensions of body awareness (image, behavior, affect, meaning) do you notice?...

REFLECTIONS
COMPANION WORKBOOK/JOURNAL

WHAT'S DIFFERENT?

Advanced Level Somatic Dimensions
Noticing Inner Experience

Refer to the expanded list of examples in Figure 13 (below) to describe your inner experience (aka, interoception) or add your own.

Airy	Emotion(s)	Image(s)	Softening
Breath	Expansive	Lukewarm	Softer
Brisk	Fluid	Melting	Smooth
Buzzing	Glowing	Oblong	Snug
Calmer	Grounded	Pulsing	Spacious
Comfy	Heart Beating	Relaxed	Tepid
Cooler	Heavier	Round	Tingling
Color(s)	Held	Settled	Vibrating
Dense	Hotter	Slower	Warmer

Fig. 13

Use the *Companion Workbook* or journal to answer these questions:

Before this ritual, my body's experience was...
After this ritual, my body is more/less...
See if you can notice *where* in the body you feel different...

All these dimensions are examples of what *possibly* can happen. It's important to accept whatever is showing up for *you*. If it's sensation, fantastic. You don't need to have more than that although, more than likely, you will begin to notice an emotional *response*. You may experience weeping, anger, or joy. You may feel calmer, more relaxed, spacious, safe, or settled. You may never be an image-oriented person or see colors, shapes or become deeply attuned to temperature or weight changes. You may never notice changes in your behaviors or experience meaning through interoception rituals. If that's the case, it's perfectly fine. Whatever is available to you is more than enough—your job is to work with whatever shows up without judging or censoring it.

Balancing Vagal Tone

We talked about the Soul Nerve in Part One (the vagus nerve) and its central importance as the communicating force between the nervous system and the brain. It's hard to overstate the importance of the vagus nerve—the largest bundle of nerves in the body. The regulation (or lack thereof) of the nervous system directly affects our decision-making process in large and small ways: from whom to marry, where to live, what career path to follow, how to vote or what to have for lunch.

Vagal tone is the activity of the vagus nerve. A high vagal tone is associated with lower blood pressure, improved blood-sugar regulation, improved digestion, better mood, reduced anxiety, and reduced risk of stroke and cardiovascular disease. A properly functioning vagus nerve also balances the nervous system, carries information from the brain to the gut (and the gut to the brain), lowers heart rate, and modulates fear, stress, and anxiety. It also regulates your breathing, creating a feeling of ease and relaxation when you breathe deeply. Perhaps the two greatest benefits of higher vagal tone is the ability to relax faster after stress and increase your immune system's ability to protect you from disease.

But when the vagus nerve senses a threat (real or perceived), it creates imbalance and dysregulates critical functions such as breathing, channeling the energy towards protecting you from danger. That's why people find themselves taking short, shallow breaths when they're in distress. When the nervous system is in a survival state, instructions dictated by the vagus nerve can grip your lungs, so that your breathing becomes more strained. Your heart rate will go up or down, depending on how the vagus nerve perceives a threat. It will also affect the function of other major organs, such as the kidneys and the digestive system (see Figure 14).

Compromising the vagus nerve pulls us out of our window of resilience and propels us into heightened levels of stress and anxiety—or shutdown—as the body desperately seeks to bring itself back into balance. If the system stays in a chronic state of survival, the body will continue to channel its defenses against the threat and away from the essential life-affirming systems, such as the immune system's ability to fight off disease.

Vagus Nerve
Latin vagus ("*wandering nerve*")

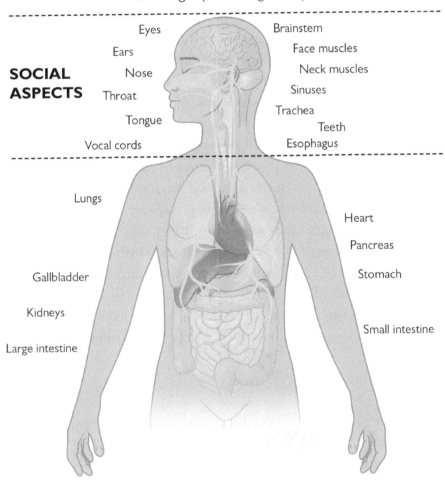

Eyes

Ears

SOCIAL ASPECTS

Nose

Throat

Tongue

Vocal cords

Brainstem

Face muscles

Neck muscles

Sinuses

Trachea

Teeth

Esophagus

Lungs

Heart

Pancreas

Gallbladder

Stomach

Kidneys

Small intestine

Large intestine

Fig. 14

So how can we regain control of the vagus nerve? Orienting is one practice that serves to bring the vagus nerve back into balance—particularly the social aspects of this bundle of nerves (Figure 14).

Advanced Level Ritual: Orienting

Orienting engages the upper part of our vagus nerve—the social portion that supplies nerves to the facial muscles and throat. In primitive times, orienting meant we were scanning our environment to identify threats lurking in the tall grass. We still have that same threat bias driving us when we're under stress, scanning for the paper tigers lurking in the grasslands of our imaginations. Orienting is a ritual we should be repeating to help soften our negativity bias and strengthen our felt sense of safety.

If you have any form of social anxiety—whether that's in intimate relationships, one-on-one, in groups or presenting in front of a crowd—you get anxious because this part of the vagus nerve perceives threat instead of recognizing a social situation where you are welcome. Here's how you change socially and shift from threat to safety. As with all the rituals you're learning, slow yourself way down. The slower the pace, the better. That's what's going to support you in coming back into your window of resilience.

Orienting Ritual:

- Go to a place—indoors or outdoors—where you find your surroundings pleasing. Perhaps a garden or sunroom. Begin by breathing slowly and mindfully. Now, *let your eyes lead you* to wherever they wish to go. When your eyes naturally land on something pleasant, have them focus on just a small portion of what you see (e.g., not the whole tree or plant or picture, but a small part, like the leaf or something within the picture) so that your eyes can fully rest into the part without straining to see more.
- Using the leaf as an example, allow your eyes to observe it in detail: Notice the color of the leaf, its shape, the way it dances in the sunlight or sways with the wind. Now take this aware-

ness inside your body and notice what's different (here's interoception again!). Take your time.

- Hang out with the body's internal sensations as you allow your eyes to gaze upon the object. Continue with this ritual for three to five minutes…or more if you find it restorative.

Depending on how much you need to repeat this practice, stay with it for as long as necessary. Over time, this ritual will help you stay calm and grounded in situations where you might normally experience social anxiety. Because the root causes of anxiety can be multifaceted, you may find that other exercises/rituals are more beneficial for a one situation or another. Experiment! You can also view the "Orienting" demo at IrisInstitute.com

(see chart on following page)

REFLECTIONS
COMPANION WORKBOOK/JOURNAL

WHAT'S DIFFERENT?

Advanced Level Somatic Dimensions
Noticing Inner Experience

Refer to the examples in Figure 15 (below) to describe your inner experience (aka, interoception), use the Glossaries of Somatic Dimensions and Emotions in the Appendix or add your own:

Airy	Emotion(s)	Image(s)	Softening
Breath	Expansive	Lukewarm	Softer
Brisk	Fluid	Melting	Smooth
Buzzing	Glowing	Oblong	Snug
Calmer	Grounded	Pulsing	Spacious
Comfy	Heart Beating	Relaxed	Tepid
Cooler	Heavier	Round	Tingling
Color(s)	Held	Settled	Vibrating
Dense	Hotter	Slower	Warmer

Fig. 15

Use the *Companion Workbook* or journal to answer these questions:

Before this ritual, my body's experience was...
After this ritual, my body is more/less...
See if you can notice *where* in the body you feel different...

Advanced Level Ritual: "Voo" Breathing Method

The next ritual that we'll be learning is an advanced practice developed by Dr. Peter Levine, as part of his Somatic Experiencing® model. Dr. Levine developed a practice to balance the nervous system, which resets the connection between the vagus nerve and other critical organs. This exercise is known as the "Voo" breathing method.

The "Voo" breathing method vibrates the vagus nerve and, over time, increases regulation. Think of it as giving this very important nerve—the longest in the body and one that sends and receives messages from almost all your major organs—a gentle massage. Here's how it works:

Begin by finding a comfortable place to sit. Close your eyes or cast them downward. Place one hand on your heart space, the other on your belly. Now, follow the breathwork ritual from earlier in this chapter and repeated here:

Use long, deep breathing as you inhale through your nose and exhale through your mouth. Put some space between the top and bottom teeth, checking to ensure the tongue is resting on your lower palette.

On the next outbreath, make the sound: "Voo"

As you exhale, use the lower register of your voice to make the sound, bringing the vibration down as far as you can into your belly or your chest. That vibration is what's releasing the vagus nerve's grip, right down the center line of your body. If you use the lower register of your voice, it's going to deepen your connection to that vibration further down into your body. Imagine you are almost making the sound of a foghorn, guiding ships to safety. As you do, pay attention to the vibration you feel inside, right underneath your hands.

Repeat this breathing method up to five total repetitions of "Voo" breathing. No more than that. If you find yourself a bit lightheaded, take gentle breaths in between or cut back to three repetitions. Go gentle and slow with this ritual.

On the final outbreath, repeat the words, at whisper-level volume, "I am safe," cascading the resonance of these words all the way down into your belly. Using this phrase will help seal the relationship between body and mind.

REFLECTIONS
COMPANION WORKBOOK/JOURNAL

WHAT'S DIFFERENT?

Advanced Level Somatic Dimensions
Noticing Inner Experience

Refer to the examples in Figure 16 (below) to describe your inner experience (aka, interoception), use the Glossaries of Somatic Dimensions and Emotions (see appendix), or add your own:

Airy	Emotion(s)	Image(s)	Softening
Breath	Expansive	Lukewarm	Softer
Brisk	Fluid	Melting	Smooth
Buzzing	Glowing	Oblong	Snug
Calmer	Grounded	Pulsing	Spacious
Comfy	Heart Beating	Relaxed	Tepid
Cooler	Heavier	Round	Tingling
Color(s)	Held	Settled	Vibrating
Dense	Hotter	Slower	Warmer

Fig. 16

Use the *Companion Workbook* or journal to answer these questions:

Before this ritual, my body's experience was ...
During this ritual, I noticed...
After this ritual, my body is more/less..
Now identify *where* in the body you feel different...

"Voo" breathing vibrates the vagus nerve so that it helps reset its communication with the organs and calms the body. **The benefits of this one single practice are so important that I'd suggest putting this practice at the top of your daily, to-do list.** Here are some of the potential rewards for "Voo'ing"!:

- Boosts your immune system's ability to fight off disease— yesssss!!!
- Balances the nervous system's giddy up and rest parts, improving resilience and regulation
- Enhances vocalization, which impacts feeling safe to speak up, to find your voice, to advocate for yourself, take up more space in the world, prioritize yourself, and reduce social anxiety
- Improves your confidence, your ability to trust your instincts, and connects you to the release of emotions, such as healthy anger, grief, joy, gratitude and so on!

I could go on, but I think these are awfully convincing benefits to encourage you to "Voo" away!

Advanced Level Rituals: Upregulating and Downregulating

Is your body prone to sympathetic or parasympathetic charge? If/when you run on high energy or anxiety (sympathetic), work your parasympathetic edges by practicing any of the downregulating rituals listed in Figure 17. If you have trouble sleeping at night, do the "Voo" breath or take a warm bath, so that you are more calm before you go to bed. Humming or laughter is a release, so it's going to help calm you, too.

If/when you run low on energy, work your sympathetic edges by practicing the upregulating rituals. Here in Figure 17 is a short list of examples and by no means is this list meant to be exhaustive. But if you get the idea of the types of exercises and rituals that will benefit you, you can add to the list based on your personal needs.

Practice one or more of the rituals listed in Figure 17 at least three to five times a week for at least a week before moving to the next practice. Listen to your body. What is giving you more energy or more calm?

RITUALS TO IMPROVE VAGAL TONE	
OVERALL BALANCE: "VOO" BREATHING	
UPREGULATE *for more energy*	DOWNREGULATE *for more calm*
Beginning rituals from Ch 6 (running or jumping in place to increase heart rate)	Intermediate and Advanced rituals from Ch 6 (e.g., interoception rituals)
Focusing on inbreath	Focusing on outbreath
Tongue on roof of mouth	Tongue on lower palette
Aerobic exercise, including running, jumping, hiking or other high impact workouts	Noticing gravity beneath you Chanting "I am safe" on the outbreath
Dancing	Calming music
Smelling something pleasant	Restorative yoga, qigong, tai chi
Singing	Humming, laughter
Cold showers	Warm blanket, bath, tea
Social contact	Walk in nature

Fig. 17

If you find your energy rising (edgy, agitated, restless) or dropping (yawning, sleepy, low energy) outside of the optimal zone, just do a practice from the opposite regulation strategy. Since this is not an exact science, if you experience the opposite of what you were seeking, try something else. Everyone is different. Experiment!

Advanced Level Ritual: Loving all of You

You want others to love all of you—the good, the bad, and the ugly—but you cannot ask that of other people without loving all of yourself first. We have this unrealistic image of who we should be and how we should look, constantly judging ourselves and scrutinizing every inch of our bodies. It is cruel how we treat the gift of having a body which, in return for all it does to keep us alive, we don't show much appreciation for it, often taking it for granted, and seemingly ignoring how much it does to keep us alive and thriving every second of our lives.

This exercise is a *love letter to your body*. Take some time to share with your body how much you appreciate it—both inside and out. For example, your beautiful hair, eyes, smile, and skin, but also specifics about how much you appreciate having legs to take you places, hands to create beauty or to touch another being, and eyes to see beauty. Inside, there's a whole world happening to keep you thriving—a heart beating, the lungs breathing every second, blood circulating through your body, and so on.

Take some time to write the love letter your body always wanted to receive from you. Once you have the letter, take some time to ground yourself, then *slowly* whisper the words out loud, from your chest or belly, allowing each word to land in your heart space (like you learned from the "Voo" breathing method).

Here is an example:

Dear Beautiful Body,

I want to express my deepest respect and gratitude for all that you do— and have— done for me. It is very important to me that you fully receive these words because I mean all of them, from the deepest places inside of me, from the depths of my soul. Thank you for...

My breath, yes thank you, for this breath, for the breath before this one and the breath after this one, so that I can breathe into you once more, so that I can remember to be present for every moment.

My heart, for each moment that it is beating— so that I can love you for another moment, another day.

My eyes, so that I can admire this beautiful world around me and admire all of you, beautiful body.

My legs, so that I can dance with you and feel the joy inside of every moment I'm moving.

My arms, so that I can hold you and hold those I love so dearly.

My mind, so that I can stay connected to you, remember you, and imagine all that I have in my life.

Through you, beautiful body, I can see, touch, smell, taste, and listen to the beauty in the world.

You are lovingly carrying me through this lifetime— through all of its highs and lows.

I am grateful I have you; Without you, I couldn't delight in this life I've been given.

You are beauty. - You are my lifelong companion. - You are the container for my soul. - I love all of you.

REFLECTIONS
COMPANION WORKBOOK/JOURNAL

WHAT'S DIFFERENT?

Advanced Level Somatic Dimensions
Noticing Inner Experience

Refer to the examples in Figure 18 (below) to describe your inner experience (aka, interoception), use the Glossaries of Somatic Dimensions and Emotions (see appendix), or add your own:

Airy	Emotion(s)	Image(s)	Softening
Breath	Expansive	Lukewarm	Softer
Brisk	Fluid	Melting	Smooth
Buzzing	Glowing	Oblong	Snug
Calmer	Grounded	Pulsing	Spacious
Comfy	Heart Beating	Relaxed	Tepid
Cooler	Heavier	Round	Tingling
Color(s)	Held	Settled	Vibrating
Dense	Hotter	Slower	Warmer

Fig. 18

Use the *Companion Workbook* or journal to answer these questions:

Before this ritual, my body's experience was ...
During this ritual, I noticed...
After this ritual, my body is more/less..
Now identify *where* in the body you feel different...

Commitment to Practice

Start with one ritual from this chapter that you'd like to repeat daily. Build it into an existing routine to make it easier to remember (e.g., after you brush your teeth, before you shower or drink your morning coffee, when you turn off your computer for the day). I'd suggest staying with the ritual until the change you experience is demonstrably different for you. Only then do I suggest moving on to another ritual from this chapter. All the rituals presented have something profound to offer. But you will only get the full benefits if you perform the ritual enough times to begin embodying the changes that result from repeated practice.

You can track your progress using the "What's Different" approach found throughout this chapter and in the *Companion Workbook*. If you need additional support, I encourage you to take advantage of the tools (demos and guided recordings, worksheets, and more) found at IrisInstitute.com.

REFLECTIONS

WHAT'S CLEARER?

After reading this chapter, what's clearer to you that you want to be sure and remember? Write your thoughts down in the *Companion Workbook* or in your personal journal.

Get the Companion Workbook @ IrisInstitute.com

IMPORTANT

Before we move to the next chapter, this is a good time to remind you that childhood trauma is not something that we can heal from an exercise. Fear and anxiety that arise from childhood trauma take time and support with a licensed professional who is trained in trauma therapy. Read through the next chapter and if you're unsure whether you are ready to do these exercises, please feel free to skip them. Instead, take loving care of yourself and refer to the resources I referenced in the preface of this book.

> **"**
> *If you want to fly, you have to give up the things that weigh you down.*
>
> - Toni Morrison

STOP SHRINKING YOURSELF TO
FIT PLACES YOU'VE OUTGROWN

CHAPTER SEVEN

Healing Childhood Wounds

Reflecting on childhood, most people can recall experiencing some form of trauma or stress that interrupted their well-being in some way. That's normal. Life isn't a perfect journey. Healing that trauma requires that you distinguish between the memories of what happened in the past and the life that you're living in the present moment. That can be a tricky thing to do; oftentimes the emotional impact of your memories doesn't leave room for much distinction between what happened 20 years ago and what happened yesterday. But it's possible to change that by healing the parts of you that are still wounded from things that may have happened decades earlier.

We know that when a baby is born, the first two months of its life essentially shape the baby's imprint of the world. We also know that human development today is much the same as it was in primitive times. A baby born into the world thousands of years ago needed her survival strategies to kick in first. That's why the right brain—where our survival strategies form—is the dominant conduit though which children still navigate childhood today.

It's not until our teenage years that the thinking brain (neo-cortex) begins to catch up and then fully matures in our mid-twenties. It's in these in-between, youthful years that we can feel invincible and often still lack the full ability to make solid, logical decisions. It is no coincidence that I often have clients in their late twenties or early thirties come into therapy for the first time, when they start reflecting on their childhood with more of an adult perspective. Suddenly, they're able to see things that happened to them years before from the vantage point of their wise adult brain. They suddenly recognize that some of what they experienced in childhood wasn't normal but, in fact, traumatic and/or abusive. They also begin to see the full impact of those experiences in their adult lives.

Mark's Story

For example, I had a man in his early thirties named Mark (not his real name) who came to see me. Mark grew up in a middle-class neighborhood. By all accounts, he was a very well-adjusted person. But Mark came to me feeling deeply insecure about himself. He'd battled addiction for years and had finally recovered by developing a strong spiritual practice and a deep connection to his twelve-step program. Yet, Mark still couldn't get past his belief that his parents saw him as a failure. As a result, he judged himself harshly and had an overactive inner critic.

Mark felt a desperate need to please others that he couldn't shake loose. He sought out work, relationships, and friendships that he believed would validate him. Objectively, Mark had all the trappings of success. He had money, an impressive career in high tech, a fancy car, a loving girlfriend, and his colleagues admired him. But Mark didn't see himself as successful or worthy. He believed that his efforts to improve his life were backfiring. Instead of feeling proud of his accomplishments, he felt more and more insignificant and incapable.

Over and over, Mark's mind told him, *I'm a failure. I'm a loser. I'm unlovable. I can't please anyone. I'm not good enough. I'm not achieving. I'm worthless.* When he came to see me, he was preparing to end his relationship with his girlfriend. Mark loved his girlfriend, but she didn't fit the impressive "ideal" that he believed everyone else expected from him. After he ended the relationship, he realized with regret how much the woman had meant to him. This led us to one of our most important breakthroughs. For the first time, Mark began to re-evaluate his life from an internal, rather than an external, lens.

Mark had always believed that if he wasn't "adding value," he was useless. Conversely, if he was successful, people would love him. We all want to feel loved. But Mark's desire to win people's approval stemmed from unhealed childhood wounds, which clouded his judgment and prevented him from going after what he truly wanted in life. His fixation reached the point where he started to lie to people, being dishonest about his feelings, beliefs, and his accomplishments. He would embellish, telling people that he'd achieved a certain standing at work, when it wasn't true. He wouldn't correct people if they said something flattering—but false—about him. The insecurity and the lies increased until he felt trapped by them.

Underneath, Mark really was a genuine person and behaving inauthentically felt terribly uncomfortable for him. In our first year of his therapy, Mark and I explored his relationships and the messages that shaped him. What messages did he believe about himself that he wanted to hold onto? Unfortunately, there were very few positive messages at the start. But one he appreciated most was how talented he was as a painter and musician. Then, we examined the beliefs about himself that he wanted to leave behind. There were many. But Mark grappled with two particularly painful beliefs that had haunted him for most of his life: *I'm a disappointment to my parents* and *I'm unworthy of happiness.*

We discussed the ways that these false messages sent him in directions that weren't in service of what he really wanted to do in the world, which included working for himself and not for a big tech company. As time passed and Mark started to feel more confident by focusing on his gifts, he began to initiate honest conversations with his parents about the challenges and struggles he'd been experiencing.

Contrary to what his fear-brain had been telling him, his parents fully supported his efforts to change his life. They celebrated him for being honest and authentic—not the fraudulent idea of the person he believed he needed to be. In the end, Mark changed careers. He started his own business, which continues to be successful and brings him great personal fulfillment. And Mark not only reunited with his girlfriend, he also married her, and they are expecting their first baby. He continues to see me for a session from time-to-time and it's always a pleasure to see him.

Children do their best to survive childhood. Still, sometimes caregivers don't meet certain needs the child has. For example, some children don't get a lot of support in learning life skills—how to study, how to stay on top of their homework, etc. Their parents may be working full time, so the children have had to figure things out for themselves, such as how to cook, clean, and get themselves dressed in the morning.

For adults who grew up this way, it can sometimes be hard to receive support from other people. Because they're so fiercely independent, when responsibilities such as children or a high-pressured job (or both) overwhelm them, they struggle to ask for help.

They aren't practiced at it. The result of holding onto these old psychological wounds can be isolating; they lose the intimate connection that people get when they allow themselves to be vulnerable enough to ask others for help.

When we're not practiced at getting our needs met from others, it can deeply impact our adult well-being. The task is to recognize and root out false, harmful beliefs that stem from unhealed wounds. By replacing those false beliefs with new convictions that are truthful, uplifting, and inspiring, we can move toward our fullest and most courageous selves.

Advanced Level Rituals: Cultivating Healthy Beliefs
False Beliefs (Introjects)

So, how do you begin to identify your false beliefs? It starts by learning to distinguish between what's *really* true about you and the *false* beliefs you were conditioned to accept, also called introjects. *Introjects are ideas, attitudes or beliefs that are unconsciously adopted from other people such as parents, peers, teachers, social and cultural networks, or the media.* Introjects are a defense mechanism, first defined by Sigmund Freud, which occur when a person internalizes the voice of an external authority figure, such as a parent. The child will identify with that outside influence so strongly and intensely that he internalizes the introject as truth. For example, a father telling his son: "boys don't cry" and the boy never cries again. This is an example of an introject and—I might add—a powerful and destructive one.

Introjects can also be positive and life-affirming. But when they're negative, they can lead to experiences like Mark's, where the psychological wounds run so deep that they impact every area of one's life. We can heal false beliefs by swapping them for healthy beliefs that accurately reflect who we are today and strengthen our sense of self-worth. We do that through the repetition of saying what is true (or what we want to be true) about ourselves until the body and mind fully inhabit the new, healthy belief.

Swap in Healthy Beliefs

Look at the following list. As you reflect on your childhood, think about what introjects or messages are still shaping your attitudes and beliefs about yourself. Circle the ones that remain part of your present life. Divide these messages into two categories—ones you want to hold on to that serve you and the ones you want to leave behind.

WHAT MESSAGES HAVE SHAPED YOU?
Circle all that apply

FALSE BELIEFS - *Introjects*	HEALTHY BELIEFS
SHAME	**CONFIDENCE**
I should have known better	I did the best I could
I should have done something	I do/did what I can with what I've got
I did something wrong	I do/did my best
I am to blame	I am not at fault
I cannot be trusted	I am trustworthy
My best is not good enough	I do my very best
ADVERSE SOCIAL/ FAMILIAL NORMS	**NOURISHING SOCIAL/ FAMILIAL NORMS**
Anger is bad, scary, and not safe	I am angry
Never show you're afraid	I am afraid
Race/gender determine intelligence	I am you
Emotions are meant to be hidden	I am expression
We don't talk about painful events	I am in pain
Grief is painful; crying is weak	I am free to grieve
We must be strong	I am delicate
Vulnerability is weak	I am courageous

FALSE BELIEFS - *Introjects*	HEALTHY BELIEFS
You can't trust people	I am discerning
People are dangerous	I am safe

UNCERTAINTY & ANXIETY	CHOICE & AGENCY
I cannot trust myself	I trust myself
I am not in control	I am influential
I must be perfect	I am fluid
I must please everyone	I please me
I am weak	I am assertive
I am trapped	I am liberated
I have no options	I am flexible

IMMOBILIZED	EMPOWERED
I cannot get what I want	I am assertive
I cannot handle it/stand it	I am resilient
I cannot succeed	I am success
I cannot stand up for myself	I am my voice
I cannot let it out	I am a force
I am helpless	I am powerful

SCARCITY	ABUNDANCE
I am not good enough	I am more than enough
I am a bad person	I am good
I am terrible	I am sacred
I am damaged	I am whole
I am defective	I am exquisite
I am worthless/inadequate	I am 100% worthy
I am insignificant/unimportant	I am significant/I matter
I deserve only bad things	I deserve abundance
I am stupid	I am smart
I am an outsider	I belong

FALSE BELIEFS - *Introjects*	HEALTHY BELIEFS
I am different	I am special
I am a failure	I am success -vs- successful
I am alone	I am rooted
BODY SHAMING	**BEAUTY & SELF APPRECIATION**
I am ugly	I am exquisite
My _____ is too big	I am just the right size
My _____ is too small	I am stunning
I am too _____	I am just right
I wish I was _____	I am beautiful just as I am
Other _____	Other _____
Other _____	Other _____
Other _____	Other _____

First, take a few minutes to simply celebrate the ones you circled on the right—the ones you do already and want to take with you! I applaud you for acknowledging how awesome you are, as you are (big applause!). Take a bow or pat yourself on the back! Yayyyy!

Okay, we can move on now...

In each section above look at the beliefs you circled in the left column. Draw an arrow to the corresponding statements on the right (or one you prefer). Start with the mantra you most want to be true from the *right column.* We will work with it next.

"I Am" Mantras

Taken from Sanskrit, mantras are affirmations you say to yourself that motivate and inspire you. The next part of this ritual demonstrates how to use mantras based on the healthy beliefs (right column) you circled above.

Mantras for this ritual will begin with the two most powerful words ever spoken: I am. In the English language, this is also how we can speak something into existence that hasn't happened yet. We can put it into *present tense.*

"I am" should be spoken from a sacred part of you—right in the center of your heart space—that is aligned with your Infinite Source. With your mantra, you are speaking your wishes into existence, into the *present* moment, as if you are already *that.* In speaking what you wish for into the present, what you desire is already your reality. So, what is *that* for you?

Your mantra can be more than a counter to the false beliefs from above. It can be things such as: *I am vitality, I am aliveness, I am loved, I am enough, I am whole. I am thriving. I am ease.* Ignore being grammatically correct—your body doesn't care. There's power when we *inhabit* the words in our bodies, so for example, say "I am perfect health" is usually more powerful than saying "I am *in* perfect health." See what lands better in your body. You want your mantra synonymous with your highest self—your Original Blueprint®.

If your mantra *doesn't* begin with "I am" that's okay, too. Whatever pithy statement resonates most for you is just right.

Advanced Level Ritual: "I Am" Mantra

With your "I am" mantra in place, we'll begin with this ritual by finding a comfortable space to sit. Read these instructions in their entirety before beginning:

Place your right hand on your heart space, right in the center of your chest. Place your left hand on your belly. Gently close your eyes and repeat your mantra on each outbreath—*slowly* (!!!) repeating it at a whisper level and feeling it land in your chest each time.

Each time you say your mantra, speak your words into your

heart space by using the lower register of your voice (just like the "Voo" breathing), keeping your attention there as you *slowly* repeat your mantra, and as you notice what feels different in your body. In doing so, you are rewiring neural pathways and making your highest wishes align with the purest expression of your soul—your Original Blueprint®.

Repeat this ritual at night until you notice yourself fully inhabiting the mantra (when the mantra feels 100% true). As you recite your mantra, it's sometimes helpful to use Mala beads (sold at IrisInstitute.com) whose origins date as far back as 3,000 years ago in the traditions of Buddhism, Hinduism, and yoga. I use them, and *slowly* repeat the mantra, using my thumb and index finger to count each of the 108 beads until I come back to the start. Once you start to feel that this mantra has become part of you, choose another from your list and begin saying that mantra to yourself at night. Take your time repeating it. It's better to repeat it five times, really slowly and let it deeply land in your body than to say it a hundred times from your head. If it's one you are passionate to have fully integrated in you, try repeating it 10-15 times daily until you reach muscle memory (300 repetitions) or embodied (3,000 repetitions) or stop when you trust yourself that you've got it.

Here is an example (Figure 19) of one of my client's creative ways to write her list of mantras, which she repeated over time until each one felt 100% embodied:

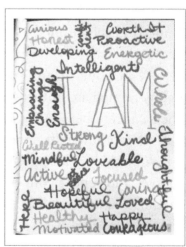

Fig. 19

Complete the ritual by answering "What's different?" You can download the "What's Different" worksheets from IrisInstitute.com. As you go, look for changes in your mood, body sensations and behavior. As with all the rituals you'll learn in this book, keep track of where it's beginning to show up in your life in the next two to four weeks. You may be surprised to notice the subtle change or even the absence of the old feeling you had about yourself!

Advanced Level Ritual: Befriend the Inner Critic

We all have an inner critic. Essentially, this is the part of us that has internalized the false messages or introjects mentioned earlier. To reinforce your healthy mantras, you can establish a different kind of relationship with your inner critic—one that swaps out the false beliefs your inner critic says to you with healthy ones. Doing this helps differentiate the inner critic from you. Because the inner critic is *not you*. It's a little introject gremlin that tries to convince you that all the unhealthy, limiting beliefs about you are true. Silly thing!

People generally form an inner critic by the age of five, especially children who live with a demeaning, demanding or abusive parent. In childhood, the voice of the inner critic generally consists of messages that we've overheard from our parents, conversations we've heard from peers or ideas we've adopted from our social networks or the media—just like all the other false beliefs we've internalized!

A young girl may say to herself, *I'm fat,* for example. But where did she first get that idea? Human beings have an evolutionary bias toward negativity that's directly linked to our bias toward threat. We're always looking to see, *where's the threat?* So, if I'm afraid of being fat, I may say to myself, *What's the worst thing that could happen to a person who's fat?* Well, if you really string that thought out all the way to its max, the fear is, *I'm going to be isolated. People will reject me. I'm unlovable and I'm alone. I'll disappear, be ostracized, or wither away and die.* The inner critic is the voice we take on when we don't feel safe in the world and its voice often has a catastrophic resonance to it.

To change this, we can forge a new relationship with the inner critic. Asking it to be quiet, beating it up or asking it to go away doesn't often work for people. Rather than trying to do away with the inner critic, we can meet it with kindness and play. The inner critic is afraid; it needs to experience more safety, more levity, more humor. So, befriend it!

Reassure your inner critic that you have better ways to handle life now as an adult. Their only job is to play and to laugh and to enjoy themselves. Play is what this hyper-vigilant inner critic wants more than anything else. Play equates to safety: *If I can play, then I'm safe. There's nothing lurking behind me ready to pounce. There isn't anything that I must do to protect myself. I can let down my defenses. I can relax and enjoy life.* Check it out—can you notice in your body how it just felt to read these words? Try again—you should feel a settling inside. If you felt something, it's already working.

One of my clients drew a picture of her inner critic and named the grumpy lady "Miss Esther." I encouraged the client to have a conversation with Miss Esther. With eyes closed, one hand on her heart space and one hand on her belly, the client called Miss Esther forward and spoke to her with loving kindness. In her mind's eye, the client said words to the effect of, *"You know what, Miss Esther, my sweetheart? Thank you so much for trying to keep me safe. I have better ways to handle these kinds of issues now. I'd love it if you and I just play together. Let's dance."*

What can you do to relate to your version of Miss Esther with more kindness and play? Maybe tickle your own Miss Esther. Imagine that you are the only one who can make your inner critic laugh. Then, any time you hear your inner critic's voice, you can say, *"Oh, we're fine. Don't sweat it. Keep playing, dancing, and laughing. We're safe. I've got you, no matter what."*

Over time, the relationship between you and your inner critic will change. You'll no longer be tempted to try to silence, punish or correct the inner critic. Instead, she becomes a supportive companion—your inner buddy and best cheerleader.

Now you know that the childhood messages you've internalized are perceived fears, not real ones. As such, they can be handled with a lighter, sweeter touch.

Here we go!

a) Draw a picture of your inner critic. It doesn't even have to be a person. It can be an entity. It could be a little gremlin, a funny monster, or a swirl of colors. For this exercise, it's not somebody you know and it's not yourself. Otherwise, whatever you want it to be is great. No need to over-think it. This isn't art class! You can always change it later if you want.

b) Name it something funny that you'll remember, so that your mind and body begin to see it as something separate from you. Don't over-think it. Again, you can change it later if you want.

c) Interoception: Close your eyes, place a hand on your heart space and a hand on your belly. Begin long, deep, slow breathing, keeping your attention in your chest and/or belly. Call your inner critic (out loud) by name. Imagine it. See how it's feeling in this moment. Is it worried? Angry? Irritated? Crabby? Now, speak to your inner critic (ideally, out loud—even if it's just at whisper volume) with kindness, knowing that the inner critic's intention is to keep you safe. Tell your inner critic something like, *"I know you're trying to keep us safe, but I have better ways to handle these issues now. All you need to do is be supportive by playing, laughing, and enjoying life with me. I've got you, no matter what happens!"*

d) Imagine doing something with the inner critic to start him on that path. Use your wildest imagination—dance with the critic, tickle him until he laughs, tell him something to bring more levity to his life. Stay with him until you notice your body loosening or settling and your inner critic becomes a playful, supportive, loving ally.

e) You can repeat this ritual any time you find yourself experiencing internal conflict. If you ever find it difficult to change the inner critic's mood or words, it's possible you need to get your body more engaged. Try *actually* dancing to music or moving your body in some playful way, as you imagine the critic's transformation. Closing your eyes or casting the eyes downward while you do this may help, too.

Most of all, your inner critic wants to feel safe. If nothing else, use words of reassurance to help him settle, like *I've got you. You are safe. I will protect you. You can rest.*

Advanced Level Ritual: Getting Needs Met as Adults

Without healing the wounds from the past, many people will (unconsciously seek unhealthy relationships, finding themselves attracted to those who will help them repeat the very same patterns they're trying to avoid. To change that, it's necessary to at least partially fulfill these needs for *oneself* first. Then healthy friendships and partnerships built on love and support (rather than the attempt to fill a void) can blossom.

Even under the best circumstances, parents and surrogate parents can't always meet your developmental needs for a variety of reasons. When that happens, either your unmet needs will remain painful trigger points for you throughout your life or you can learn to re-parent yourself with the love, patience, wisdom, and compassion that you need to truly thrive. You know *precisely* what you did/didn't get—you're living with the consequences. So, you can fill those gaps better than anyone else, including your parents, surrogates, friends, and partners.

Part I: Childhood Needs

Read through the list of childhood needs on the next page (Figure 20). If you had any needs that aren't mentioned on the list, write them down in your *Companion Workbook* or personal journal.

In each category, check the box to indicate the person in your life who filled those needs for you: check "M" for mother(s), "F" for father(s), or "S" for surrogate(s) for the met needs. If **partially met,** check the "PM" box and circle the ones that were **met.**

(see chart on following page)

CHILDHOOD NEEDS

Providing Basic Needs	Learning Life Skills	Meeting Emotional Needs
Personal hygiene: wash body, brush teeth, comb hair, clean clothes	**Household chores:** laundry, cleaning room, vacuuming, cleaning dishes, cleaning bathrooms	**Attention:** quality time, tending to your moods, listening with empathy
M F S PM	M F S PM	M F S PM
Financial security: food, shelter, clothing	**Finance skills:** budgeting, managing credit cards	**Nurturing:** loving-kindness, acceptance, physical affection
M F S PM	M F S PM	M F S PM
Balanced meals: consistent, balanced meals	**Meal preparation:** learning how to cook healthy meals	**Boundaries:** respecting boundaries with self and others
M F S PM	M F S PM	M F S PM
Safety: secure home and neighborhood	**Homework:** study skills, time management, tutoring	**Unconditional love:** loving you as you are, no need to perform
M F S PM	M F S PM	M F S PM
Medical care: regular physicals, dental appointments	**Exercise:** supporting physical activity, modeling self-care	**Being cherished:** celebrating and appreciating you
M F S PM	M F S PM	M F S PM
Education: access to education	**Social:** access to family and friends for support	**Growth:** supporting and celebrating your talents
M F S PM	M F S PM	M F S PM
Transportation: rides to/from school and activities	**Spiritual:** access to nature, church, synagogue or other sacred place	**Trust and Reliability:** dependability
M F S PM	M F S PM	M F S PM

Fig. 20

First, take a moment to notice what needs **did** get met. Under the circumstances you experienced as a child, is there something one or more of your caregivers did well or reasonably well?

It's often (but not always) more common for families to meet the needs listed in the first two columns more so than the far-right column. Consistently meeting emotional needs listed on the right can be more challenging. It's very likely one or more of our needs from any of these columns remain unmet or partially met.

For example, you may look at the list and say, *"I needed my dad to cherish me."* That's valid. And if he did not meet that need, you may carry an emotional wound that causes you to struggle with feelings of unworthiness, loneliness, or isolation. You may choose unhealthy partners who reinforce these feelings of not being cherished or appreciated.

Part 2: Healing Turnarounds

While you can't undo what's happened in the past, you can change how you respond to it now. To resolve any emotional void carried over from your childhood, you can turn it around and heal yourself. Healing turnarounds put the power of healing back in your control and liberate you from relying on the people who weren't able to meet those needs for you. For example, if the need you chose was "cherished" and more specifically, *I needed my dad to cherish me,* then a healing turnaround would be: *I cherish me.*

Step 1:

From the list of childhood needs, choose one unmet need from childhood that you want to work with today. Next, complete these prompts:

- My childhood need was… [*Example: I needed my dad to cherish me*]
- Healing Turnaround: What I know to be true now is… [*Example: I cherish me*]

175

Step 2:

Now, write your healing turnaround in your own handwriting (do not type these, even if you're using the *Companion Workbook*) at least fifteen times. That movement of the hand and seeing the words in your own handwriting helps reinforce and affirm the new belief.

Step 3:

Going back to your *Companion Workbook* or personal journal, write an inventory of all the ways you already meet your healing turnaround for yourself:

Example: *My childhood need was that I wanted my dad to cherish me. I felt unlovable. I felt insecure. What I know to be true now is that **I cherish me**. How do I know that to be true? I exercise every day. I get good rest at night. I surround myself with people who love me. My dog loves me. I also tend to the things that nourish me on a weekly basis, including yoga, gardening, cooking, reading, and drawing.*

Step 4:

There's more—we need your body to get into the game now. Pull out your interoception ninja skills! Ready? Go!...

Using your healing turnaround, take some time to ground yourself. Find a comfortable chair to sit in. Close your eyes; feel your sitz bones, your feet, and your back, as you take in support from beneath and behind you. With one hand on your heart space and one hand on your belly, inhale and exhale using long, slow, deep breaths.

Slowly speak your turnaround sentence at least fifteen times, whispering the words out loud, cascading each word and letting it land in your chest/belly, until your body feels a settling inside. You can also use your Mala beads in Step 4.

Step 5:

Conclude the ritual by answering the "what's different" prompt in your *Companion Workbook* or personal journal. You can also download the "What's Different" worksheet found at Iris-Institute.com. As always, look for changes in your mood, body sensations and your behavior and keep track of where it's beginning to show up in your life in the next two to four weeks.

Repeat this ritual for each healing turnaround until each one feels true for you (take your time; this ritual may have a long shelf life!).

Being honest with yourself about your psychological wounds can be very difficult. It's human nature to avoid things that we fear will bring us pain. It may feel easier to avoid these wounds by denying or repressing them when they become too scary or painful to face. If you ever catch yourself in moments of fear, pain, avoidance, or denial, I invite you to take a breath and ask yourself: *What am I afraid of? What keeps me from exploring what's underneath the fear? Is what I'm fearing just another paper tiger? Do I need support from a trusted source?*

The beauty of healing childhood/psychological wounds is that you don't need anyone but yourself to do it. Doing the healing yourself means you will know precisely what to say. Trying to talk to your parents or the people who were part of your upbringing will be less satisfying and potentially (depending on the responses you receive) re-wounding.

You are the expert on you. You know what needs didn't get met, and how to phrase those needs. Therefore, one of the most fundamental keys to healing even the most painful psychological wounds—is your dear, sweet self.

Advanced Level Exercise: Marry Yourself

No other will be with you your entire lifetime but you. Not your parents, your spouse, your friends, not even your children will have known you for your entire lifetime. So, marry yourself first. Once you commit to yourself, you can be far more available to those you love. Be creative. Consider the commitments you wish to honor. Here is a sample vow for your marriage:

I, _____ , choose you, and your beautiful body and mind for life. I promise you my deepest love, my complete devotion and tender loving care from this moment forward. I promise to love you, commit to you, and support you. I will appreciate you as you are, care for you and keep you safe. I pledge to respect you and your abilities and to remember all that you do for me each and every moment of my life. As you do for me, I will lend you strength, encouragement, and an abiding faith in challenging times. I promise to honor you, love you and cherish you for the rest of our lives.

I celebrate you exactly as you are, beautiful body and mind. I will respect and honor you always. I will accept and love you unconditionally. Just as you are, I love you deeply. I will have and hold you through tears, laughter, sickness and in health. I will love and cherish you from this day forward, beautiful Self.

This is my sacred commitment to you. From this moment forward, we are in a union before our Infinite Source.

I love and cherish you, always, _____

Conclude this exercise by answering the "what's different" prompt in your *Companion Workbook* or personal journal (you can also download this worksheet from IrisInstitute.com). As always, look for changes in your mood, body sensations and your behavior and keep track of where it's beginning to show up in your life in the next two to four weeks.

Commitment to Practice

Focus on one ritual at a time. Keep it simple and doable. You want to be successful with whatever you choose.

Be kind to yourself. This journey isn't easy and no one is perfect. There will be setbacks but if you stay committed, you will grow.

REFLECTIONS

WHAT'S CLEARER?

After reading this chapter, what's clearer to you that you want to be sure and remember? Write your thoughts down in the *Companion Workbook* or in your personal journal.

 Get the Companion Workbook @ IrisInstitute.com

> **"**
>
> *Even after all this time the sun never says to the earth, 'you owe me.' Look what happens with a love like that. It lights up the whole sky.*
>
> - Hafiz

CHAPTER EIGHT

When "No" Fortifies Relationships

How do we preserve our relationships *and* speak our truth? How can we accept and make amends with those we've hurt? How do we take responsibility for intentionally or unintentionally wounding others? How do we live our legacy now, seeding love, joy, hope and peace wherever we go?

We "bring the weather" to our relationships and resentment is a Category 5 hurricane. Resentment happens when we've given more of ourselves than we really wanted to give. As Dr. Gabor Maté once said, "resentment is soul suicide." We keep a tally in our minds when what we give no longer accounts for what we believe we've received; we're building up a reservoir of our "good deeds" and feeling unappreciated. "Look at all the things I've done for you!" we say. If you're resentful toward someone who matters to you, it is your personal responsibility to change that by being emotionally honest, starting with yourself.

How do you know if you're resentful? Check in with your throat and chest—are you feeling constriction there? Do you find yourself ruminating, regretting giving too much of yourself to someone or something? Do you find yourself feeling envious of that person? If so, there's a good chance you've gone too far with your "yesses" and resentment has taken over. Resentment often builds when you're afraid to set clear boundaries. There's no room for any of that in your Original Blueprint®.

Aaron's Story

Take for example, my 47-year-old client Aaron (not his real name), who deeply resented his father's absence during most of his childhood. During our sessions, he easily recalled all the things that dad did wrong back then. It did not surprise me that, as an adult, he harbored similar resentments towards his wife and his boss, along with his father, for his lot in life. Using the resentment exercise, you'll learn in this chapter he began to see that much of his present-day resentment stemmed from his old desire to please his dad. He desperately wanted his father to love and pay attention to him as a child.

As an adult, the client would say "yes" to everyone. But when it came to things that he wanted or needed, he'd deny himself everything while continuing to accommodate those around him, slowly building resentment toward others but never advocating for his own needs. He was afraid he'd be abandoned or rejected— much like he experienced rejection from his father—so he refused to say "no" and continued feeling unappreciated, resentful, and envious.

My client felt miserable most of the time. At times, he even appeared to revel in his misery. He remarked, "I'm on the verge of long-term resentment toward my wife." I confronted him and said, "You have no right to be resentful toward her if you didn't honestly communicate your needs. You're responsible for putting yourself in this position by not being honest. You didn't do anyone any favors by saying "yes" to things you really didn't want. And now, your resentment is eating you up. It all starts with your relationship with your dad. I think you need to resolve those feelings first, so that you can see more clearly what you need to do today to be more present and authentic with the people in your life."

Because the therapeutic relationship was long-standing and resilient, the direct feedback I gave him shook him to his core and had him deeply reflecting on his own behavior. He took it to heart and went back to his wife, apologizing for not being more honest about his needs. The two are in couples therapy now, working through their challenges and he is far more accepting of who his father truly is and what's possible (and not possible) in the relationship with his dad.

Before we get to repairing resentment, let's begin at the origins of resentment—the importance of setting boundaries.

Advanced Level Ritual: Setting Boundaries

You'll find this ritual either easy or difficult. For some people, setting healthy boundaries by saying "no" to others is a normal part of their everyday life. For other people, setting boundaries feels excruciatingly hard.

When you don't set healthy boundaries, there's a tremendous cost to yourself and your relationships. Trust is broken—sometimes indelibly. If the people in your life don't know where they stand with you, it's confusing to them. People may become wary of engaging with you on any meaningful level because they wonder when you'll catch them off-guard, surprised that you said "yes" to something that, in reality, you didn't want or intend to do.

While your intentions may be good—perhaps wanting harmony, balance, maintaining connection or approval—you're likely to get the opposite result. Not setting boundaries will repel people from you. It's very unkind *not* to say "no" when you mean "no".

Saying "no" can (and should) be done with consideration. For example, "I'm sorry but that's not going to work for me," would suffice. "I can't do that because…", is another way to kindly say, "no." "I can't do that, but here's what I *can* do," is another. You're using kindness and diplomacy *and* being direct. Keeping healthy relationships intact requires saying "no" sometimes and prevents the building of resentment that can destroy intimate bonds.

To take care of yourself *and* your relationships, set healthy boundaries with others. Answer the questions below in your *Companion Workbook* or in your personal journal. Start with the easier situations or people and then build towards the more challenging ones in your life.

- Who is the person with whom you need to establish a clearer boundary?
- What's the situation?
- What do you normally do to stay safe in that scenario?
- What's the benefit to you?
- What's the benefit to them?
- What's the cost to you?
- What's the cost to them?
- Next time, I will instead say:

When you actually have the exchange with the person in real life, write down what you noticed leading up to, during, and after saying "no".

REFLECTIONS
COMPANION WORKBOOK/JOURNAL

WHAT'S DIFFERENT?

Advanced Level Somatic Dimensions
Noticing Inner Experience

Refer to the expanded list of examples in Figure 21 (below) to describe your inner experience (aka, interoception) or an even more expanded list in the Glossaries of Somatic Dimensions and Emotions in the Appendix:

Airy	Emotion(s)	Image(s)	Softening
Breath	Expansive	Lukewarm	Softer
Brisk	Fluid	Melting	Smooth
Buzzing	Glowing	Oblong	Snug
Calmer	Grounded	Pulsing	Spacious
Comfy	Heart Beating	Relaxed	Tepid
Cooler	Heavier	Round	Tingling
Color(s)	Held	Settled	Vibrating
Dense	Hotter	Slower	Warmer

Fig. 21

Before this experiment, my body's experience was...
During this experiment, my body's experience was...
After this experiment, my body is more/less...
See if you can identify *where* in the body you feel different...

If this experiment was difficult in any way, repeat it as a ritual, until you feel settled and able to establish boundaries more easily.

However, if the experiment triggered a response that felt intolerable, you may need the support of a trained practitioner to support you with boundary setting (refer to the book's preface for resources).

If you already knew this experiment would be too much and passed on it, that's a boundary in and of itself!

Again, I encourage you to reach out for help if you need it.

Advanced Level Ritual: Resentment-to-Acceptance

Name an authority figure (mom, dad, surrogate parent, teacher) from childhood whom you resent most.

This will be the person you will refer to for this next exercise (if you are unable to identify anyone from your childhood but you have someone in mind from your adult life, you can do this exercise using them).

Now, sometimes resentment stems from unforgivable acts, such as abuse, neglect or when a whole group of people have been systematically marginalized and abused. If that applies in your case, ask yourself if you're giving your abuser more energy than they deserve. Is the resentment you feel sucking your life force from you? If you can lift the resentment, it may free you to channel some of that energy in more productive ways—perhaps even change systems that perpetuate dysfunctional behavior like racism, sexism, antisemitism, and homophobia. Instead of attempting compassion or forgiveness (some things just simply aren't forgivable), *acceptance* may allow you to release the stuck energy that could be put to better use in your life. It's a tall order but perhaps, over time, we can lift each other up if we keep pressing forward.

Abuse and biases aside, if you resent someone from your adult life, such as an ex-wife or ex-husband, and you spend a tremendous amount of your precious time resenting them, you might as well have stayed with him or her because he or she is continuing to suck the joy from your life.

Apply the following exercise with a person you're feeling resentment toward:

Reflect on the person you resent most. Go back as far as you can to recall the earliest memory when you felt resentment or anger toward them. Complete the exercise by writing as many examples of why you resent them. You can find copies of this worksheet in the *Companion Workbook* or at IrisInstitute.com.

Here are three examples.

Example: Dad

Column 1	Column 2	Column 3	Column 4
I resent (Dad) for...	Instead (Dad) should have...	How am I different than (Dad)...	How am I similar to (Dad) (radical honesty here!)
Being completely absent from my life	Been in my life on a regular basis	I'm actively in my kids lives	I'm not similar
Working all the time	Balanced work and home life	I'm not different	I do the same thing— working late at night after my kids go to bed
Drinking and saying abusive things to me	Stopped drinking and prioritized me	I very rarely drink any alcohol	I substitute work as my addiction to avoid my painful feelings

Let's get deeply curious:

Close your eyes and imagine this person when he/she was a young child. Now imagine yourself at that same age, sitting there right next to him/her. Take your time imagining the two of you there, together as young children. Ask him/her: *Tell me how life is for you?* Listen closely to their answer. Does it give you a window into the forces that shaped his/her external and emotional life?

Write down what insights you received from this exercise. Take your time. Answer the following question:

What might've been in the way of them meeting my needs—the needs you listed in column two?

Looking at your *Companion Workbook* or personal journal entry, what are you feeling? Is it anger? Compassion? Understanding? Can you see any similarities between the two of you? Write them down.

Is your resentment or envy holding you back today? If so, how is it impacting your relationships, including with this person? What's one thing you have the power to change that would liberate you from resentment or envy in this and other relationships?

Accepting and making peace with what happened in the past—with compassion and empathy—can release you. That's what we all want for ourselves—to be accepted as we are; I find acceptance to be the most powerful antidote to resentment. If you can accept the person you resent, see him/her as flawed, just as we all have flaws (including you), it releases both of you. You can be at peace within yourself and free to live with grace.

Acceptance isn't resignation either; you're not *giving up*. You're choosing acceptance over resentment. In fact, acceptance is the opposite of giving up—it's a force multiplier. It frees up the stagnant energy to channel it into areas of your life that you want to see expand. It enables you to grow exponentially to your fullest and highest self.

Advanced Level Ritual: Making Amends

Now it's time to make amends with anyone who you regret ever hurting along the way. If you've been abused by this person in any way, I'll leave it up to you to decide if making amends would be helpful to you. I don't think we need to forgive everyone. If it's a toxic relationship, acceptance or forgiveness from afar are better antidotes.

Okay, let's take an inventory of those in your life with whom you want to make amends. From your inventory, identify the people you want to reach out to and the ones you would rather write about and keep private for yourself. If you've been through a particularly painful or traumatizing experience with someone, it may be better not to contact that person directly at this time. You may conclude that it's better to keep your distance because it would be harmful to either you or the other person. If that's the case, please don't feel pressure to make contact. The following exercise should feel safe and cathartic for *you*, without being destructive to anyone else.

Either way, if there are people you do not want to contact, you might want to take some time to read your letters to them out loud to yourself, maybe with a compassionate listener present. Each time you complete an amends with someone (written or spoken directly), ask yourself:

- How did it feel to extend a sincere apology to that person?
- Were there moments where it stretched you out of your comfort zone?
- What was it like to make peace with those you've had trouble with in the past?

Be prepared if someone you reach out to doesn't accept your desire for amends. In this case, you can complete the amends with that person in their absence.

Commitment to Practice

Watch for moments when you find yourself saying "yes" to things you don't want to do. Pay attention to the impulse, write about it and see if you can be direct and kind with that person and tell them what is—and isn't—working for you in the relationship.

REFLECTIONS

WHAT'S CLEARER?

After reading this chapter, what's clearer to you that you want to be sure and remember? Write your thoughts down in the *Companion Workbook* or in your personal journal.

Get the Companion Workbook @ IrisInstitute.com

Transition

As you know by now, any time we shift from one thing to the next—big or small—it's important to note it in our bodies. It doesn't matter if the shift is something small, like taking a break at work, while you move from one meeting to the next, or something big like planning a wedding or having a baby. It's important to take a moment to notice the transition.

First, stand up.

As we make the transition from Part Two of this book to Part Three, notice what's at your back, what's behind you. In Part Two you challenged yourself to apply what you learned through rituals and exercises. Notice what's different for you now than before you took the challenge.

Look at what's in front of you in Part Three. You'll be looking outward to take your work into the world.

Take a nice, long deep breath (inbreath through your nose, outbreath through your mouth).

Step forward.

CONGRATULATIONS!!!

You are well on your way :)
Keep up the outstanding work—you got this!!!

PART
THREE

BRINGING YOUR FIERCENESS
INTO THE WORLD

❝

Genius is in the idea. Impact, however, comes from action.

- Simon Sinek

PART THREE

Bringing Your Fierceness Into the World

Now that you have completed the inner journey to liberate yourself from fear and reclaim your Original Blueprint®, it's time to look at how we can positively affect the external world. Part Three is all about externalizing who you are in positive ways.

❝

One day you will ask me which is more important? My life or yours? I will say mine and you will walk away not knowing that you are my life.

- Khalil Gibran

TO FIND
YOURSELF
IS TO TOUCH

A WHOLE DAMN
UNIVERSE

CHAPTER NINE

Mobilizing Your Original Blueprint®

Humans are microcosms of the earth and our universe. Like the earth, we are 70% water (fluids) and 30% matter (organs). Science also has taught us that we are made from the same material as the stars in our universe. We also share 99.9% of the same DNA across gender and ethnicity; less than 0.1% of us is different from the next person. Knowing these facts tells me there's no doubt we are *One* single source of energy—what I call the *Collective You*.

Now that you have begun to reconnect with your Original Blueprint®, how will you transmit all the love you're fully embodying and share it with the world?

Until this chapter, you've been exploring yourself, how your experiences in life shaped you as an individual and how your village impacts your personal growth and development. In this chapter, you'll be turning the mirror around and looking at the *Collective You*; how your Original Blueprint® can positively impact the world. The mark you leave on the world isn't necessarily dependent on what you say or do. It's sometimes what you *don't say* and what you *don't do* that leaves an impression. Empowering your Original Blueprint® to have a positive impact on the *Collective You* is imperative to solving the most pressing issues of our time.

Virtually all the man-made problems that we face on this planet—from war to climate change to racism, sexism, and poverty—stem from people using others for their own ends (often to amass power and wealth for themselves) and ignoring the consequences that arise from their actions (or inactions). This is the opposite of how people behave when they're operating from their Original Blueprint®. True power is inseparable from personal responsibility and the commitment to being in service of the *Collective You*.

We all have positive and not-so-positive impact on the world. It takes courage and resilience to look at the unsavory sides of ourselves.

For example, many people believe we can't impact global issues, a belief that keeps us trapped in a narrow prism of the world, worrying only about ourselves and a small circle of family or friends. But, as we know, we aren't wired to be isolated. Humans are pack animals. We need each other. We need support. We are far more powerful when we come together.

With massive advances in technology in the past fifty years, the world has become much smaller than ever before. Travel, communications, technology, and other industries have made access to other people and other cultures far more accessible. Yet, we still fear "otherness." We must ask ourselves, *Why?* The truth is that our dividedness is something that we *can* change. In fact, that is one of the most crucial lessons that we must learn, as a global community, if human beings are to continue to survive and thrive on this planet.

One small contribution from you can have a butterfly effect

(*meaning:* something small happening in one part of the world—like the flap of a butterfly wing—can have a big impact, creating massive change across the planet). How you make a positive contribution will become clearer to you over time. You are in the world right now, doing some job out there that ultimately is intended to help others. From CEO to street sweeper, we are all doing the same job—we are here to help each other. Make your helping count.

When families, communities and villages are successful, the potential for emotional, spiritual, and material abundance increases exponentially. Economies grow, innovation expands, and we do not leave anyone behind. A rising tide lifts all boats, as the old saying goes. Deficit thinking is a primitive, fear-based, survival strategy that is an antiquated way of looking at society through the zero-sum lens of the Haves and the Have Nots. It's short-sighted. If we lift each other up, success and opportunity can have a multiplier effect on our collective growth.

Advanced Level Ritual: Living Your Legacy Story

Ask yourself: *What's the legacy that I want to leave for the generations to come? How do I want to leave the world better than when I entered it?*

Fully inhabiting your Original Blueprint® is not just about healing and growing for yourself or your family—it's about the legacy of your impact on the wider world. Legacy is not about the end of life; it's about **living your legacy** right now, every single day. Your legacy shouldn't be a surprise to you or anyone else when you depart the world. It should be clear as day that you've been *living your legacy* all along.

Are you convinced that you matter by now? I certainly hope so because you have a *solemn obligation* to fully participate in this world.

Writing what I call a *Legacy Story* will help you define and put your purpose into action. Write the narrative in present tense. Make it specific and actionable. Before writing that story for yourself, let's get clearer about your legacy and how you want to impact others.

First, how big do you want to go? Do you want your legacy to influence your family, community, the world? Look at this **Legacy Map** (Figure 22) to see increasing spheres of influence:

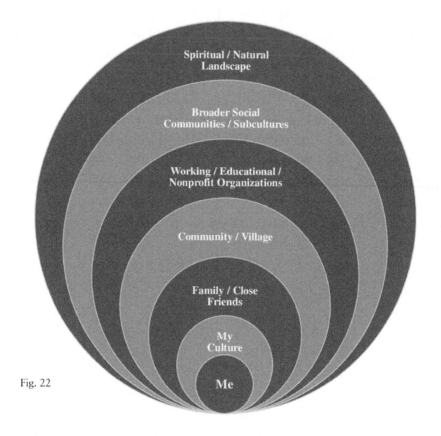

Fig. 22

Across these spheres of influence, explore the following legacy questions. For those who have children as a priority, I encourage you to also extend your answers beyond your children. Take your time, reflecting and writing your story, using these prompts to flesh out the narrative (2-3 paragraphs) in your personal journal or in the *Companion Workbook* (if you're unclear, ask a few trusted confidantes to talk it through with you or you can go to my website to refer to a Legacy Story example):

- What's your #1 superpower?
- What are you most passionate about?
- Who do you care most about?
- What's the burning need you can fulfill in the world?
- How far will you go to see it happen?
- Will its impact happen in your lifetime or in generations to follow?
- Specifically, what will be different because of your contribution?
- What resources or support do you need to make it happen?
- What might get in the way of your success? How will you overcome it?
- How will you get yourself back on track *when* (not if) you lose sight?

Advanced Level Ritual: Legacy Commitments

Complete these questions in your *Companion Workbook* or journal:

Be specific…
- In the next thirty days, I will:
- In the next sixty days, I will:
- In the next 180 days, I will:
- In a year, I will:
- In two years, I will:
- In five years, I will:
- In a decade, I will:
- Before I leave this world, my legacy will look like:
- If my legacy remains incomplete, I will ensure it continues with (name person or entity):

Everyone has the potential to be a leader; everyone can help shape the different systems of which they are a part. Look in your system—the answer to your legacy may be surprisingly close. For example, how can a CEO have a massive impact on our social systems? Prioritize diversity hires in the C-suite, mentor up-and-coming women and other marginalized professionals in the workforce, invest wealth in an underserved school and develop a pipeline of new hires from that community.

Conversely, what can someone with limited resources do? Volunteer time to disadvantaged youth as a mentor, teach in a school system that needs help or participate in a movement you care about—like combatting climate change.

You've already learned to do one of the single most impactful things that will help you define the legacy that you leave the world—you have learned how to regulate your nervous system. Going into the world with a body and mind that are working in concert means you're more likely to notice how safe you are, how others are safe, and how much the world needs you. Keep practicing that and you've already given the greatest gift you can give to the world. A nervous system that is regulated—is contagious.

Advanced Level Ritual: Vision Board—Manifesting Your Legacy

A vision board is a visual representation of your legacy and your heart's desires—an externalization of your hopes, dreams, aspirations, and intentions. By taking these dreams out of the internal patterns and systems in your head, you can bring them into an interactive field. You can invite the Universe to participate, listen, and help enact your vision. Manifesting is one of the most powerful ways to enact change in your life; it's drawing upon the sacred feminine in all of us (all genders) that doesn't require *doing* anything, it requires *being*—a powerful calling out to the Universe to make it happen for and with us.

The images, words, and phrases that you put on your board serve as a reminder of your commitments in your legacy and what you want most in life. In addition to an "I am" mantra, visualization is one of the most powerful things that you can do to bring what you want into your present reality. It's also a fun way to celebrate your commitment(s) and to create a visual representation of what you wish to manifest.

Collect magazines that represent you through imagery and words, find inspiring phrases and quotes to keep you motivated, and add the pictures of the people and things you love most. Once you have a good collection of all these items, cut them out and place them on a trifold board (like the ones kids use for science fairs). Make sure you use some form of adhesive that can be unstuck, too, so that over time, as the vision changes, you can update what you wish to see manifest. Avoid the temptation of using your computer to print out images—the journey of discovery and *taking your time* with your board is part of your healing and growth. Don't rush through this journey.

Imagine all of what you see on the board is possible and right around the corner. Begin to notice in your body where the feeling of *anticipation* resides in you. Hang out with its dimensions inside and imagine you can call all of what you want in life here into the present moment. Feel the anticipation of it coming. What you create on your vision board is sacred, so keep it where only you and your Infinite Source can see it. Trust that what you request will be answered with your highest interests in mind. Make it a sacred pact and allow it to be something that continues to transform, as you do, throughout your life. As things manifest, save the images in a folder so that you can celebrate and appreciate how far you've come, and introduce new visions to the board.

Advanced Level Ritual: Appreciation Begets Abundance

The relationship you have with your Infinite Source is very much the same as any other relationship in your life. We all want to be appreciated for our acts of love; when you appreciate your partner for their kindness or generosity, it simply encourages more of the same. Who doesn't want to be appreciated too! It makes us feel good and motivates us to do more of the same. Your relationship with the Universe is no different. It wants to know that what it's giving you is being appreciated. When you appreciate what you have—free of agendas or expectations—more goodness will come to you.

I prefer the word "appreciation" as opposed to "gratitude" because it's more active. Every day, I'm in conversation with my Infinite Source, sharing what I appreciate about the life I've been given and the abundance I experience every day. This is my most sacred relationship, the one that feeds and nourishes my soul. This dialogue comes easy to me because I have cultivated it, just like any relationship in my life that matters to me.

With my Infinite Source, I know that I am loved, no matter what. I encourage you to be in the same—or similar—dialogue: to appreciate the abundance of your life, every day. In doing so, you will find that the Universe will respond in kind with more abundance for you. As with any love in your life, when we appreciate what we have, we get more of it. It is the most powerful ritual if what you want is to manifest more of what you love about your present, exquisite life.

REFLECTIONS

WHAT'S CLEARER?

After reading this chapter, what's clearer to you that you want to be sure and remember? Write your thoughts down in the *Companion Workbook* or in your personal journal.

Get the Companion Workbook @ IrisInstitute.com

> **The path of the warrior is lifelong, and mastery is often simply staying on the path.**
>
> — Richard Strozzi-Heckler

CHAPTER TEN

Continuing the Work

As you complete this stage of your work, first let me say how much I hope this work has supported your healing and growth. Anyone who picks up a book like this tends to place high value on themselves and the life they've been given so I commend you for your incredible commitment and devotion to yourself.

Before we close, it is important that you continue this healing journey and so I am offering some recommendations for you to consider. Also, be sure to check out all the helpful tools and resources at IrisInstitute.com.

Commitment to Practice

In terms of choosing an ongoing commitment to something that keeps you connected to your Original Blueprint®, I recommend you choose one or two rituals. You should choose whichever rituals your heart desires most, but here are a few suggestions. I would also be certain that at least one of your choices engages your body.

From the chapter, *When Mind Meets Body and Falls in Love:*
- Advanced Level Ritual: Interoception—Beyond Sensation
- Advanced Level Ritual: "Voo" breathing method

From the chapter, *Healing Childhood Wounds:*
- Advanced Level Ritual: Healing Turnarounds

From the chapter, *Mobilizing Your Original Blueprint®:*
- Advanced Level Ritual: Legacy Commitment
- Advanced Level Ritual: Vision board

As you continue with your rituals, here are a few recommendations to support you:

1. **Accountability:** Choose an accountability partner—someone you live with is preferable. Be specific about how you want that person to support you (e.g., daily/weekly reminders, exactly what day and time, in person or virtual).

2. **Reflections:** Pull together any of the reflections noted at the end of each chapter that still resonate or that you want to remind yourself about in the future and take them with you.

3. **Support:** Start an Original Blueprint® group—keep it small and intimate (3-5 people is the ideal). You can use the worksheets provided on my website to get the group going—IrisInstitute. com. Personally, I have my own Original Blueprint® group of four people that meets every four to six weeks; we often use a topic from this book to explore an aspect of our Original Blueprint® each time.

> *Only those who will risk going too far can possibly find out how far one can go.*
>
> — T.S. Eliot

CONCLUSION

This is a long and challenging journey for most people. Getting this far is quite a cause for celebration. Your path is not about trying to be perfect. You're not going to close this book and be all done with this work. Becoming complacent or sliding back into old habits just allows your paper tigers to take up residence in your mind again—growling and snarling and trying to conjure up threats where none exist. No, this is the start of a lifelong journey to stay in touch with who you are in your Original Blueprint®—the part of you that embodies your mental, emotional, and spiritual integrity. This work is also about creating your legacy by challenging yourself to fully show up and be courageous in the world.

One of the most empowering goals you can set for yourself is to live fearlessly in the face of life's challenges. Everyone experiences fear, pain, and trauma at some point. Some of it is collective trauma, such as fighting through a natural disaster that strikes without warning or struggling to survive and provide for your family during hard economic times. You may wrestle with personal trauma, such as the loss of a spouse or a child. Everyone feels overwhelmed and out of control at some point. And the truth is that you can't control what happens in the world. No one can. But you can have mastery over what goes on within you. Mastery over yourself is paramount.

Imagine a majestic, thousand-year-old, redwood tree. That redwood tree has been through all kinds of changes in weather patterns. It's survived storms, lightning strikes, floods, fire—all kinds of hazards that could have destroyed it over the centuries. But that tree has endured because its stable roots keep it grounded. That mighty redwood tree has the resilience to persevere through all kinds of changes, triumphs, and crisis. It has "family" around it —due to the way redwood trees grow in pods—and it can lean on the family for support.

Collectively, a redwood family can exist for thousands of years, providing new saplings with the space to grow beneath their massive canopy of shade. The redwoods don't wait for the perfect conditions to emerge before they can grow; new life emerges even during change and upheaval. These ancient trees persist through the fires, floods, and droughts, growing stronger with each passing year.

The redwood tree is tall and solid. But it also has many smaller branches that reach up to the sun's light above. Those branches sway with the changing winds. The leaves on the branches move and tremble and fall away as the seasons change. They're not stuck. They're flexible. That flexibility allows the tree to reach toward the sun's light, taking in the nourishment it needs and generating oxygen for life to grow around it—including you.

The redwood tree is the way I see myself: I'm rooted in the ground, with my support system firmly planted around me. I have the resilience to move through any storm, any crisis or trauma. And I move through it with flexibility. I metabolize and use the energy of whatever happens, whether society brands the circumstance good or bad. It doesn't pull me off my center. In fact, I don't label things as "good" or "bad" anymore. I acknowledge any change that happens in the world and I meet it in the moment, with full presence, as much as possible. Meeting experiences as they come allows me to stay rooted in my body—grounded, connected, and alive in the moment. But I had to confront my deepest fears, over and over again and each time, allow my nervous system to settle a bit more. As time passed, I was able to hold my ground with increased resilience and cross the threshold to reunite with my Original Blueprint®. The wild ride to get here has made the reunion even sweeter.

That was not the case before I began this work. A hurricane would come through and knock all my branches down. I couldn't hold my footing when challenges or trauma rocked my life. Emotion swept me away with every crisis and I couldn't pull myself back together.

I had to *devote* myself to nurturing and continuing the process of healing my deepest wounds. I focused on regulating my nervous system, building capacity and resilience, and loving the parts of myself that were still suffering from my childhood wounds. I took responsibility for the ways that I showed up in my life and how my actions affected other people. It's been a lifelong journey to get to the point where staying open and curious has become second nature.

I challenge my fears, making it a point to travel and meet people who are vastly different from me. In doing so, I've learned how much more we are the same than different. I have stared down the caustic shame I held—from the loss of my own children to the deep-seated corners of my own many biases amassed in my DNA from the generations who've walked this earth before me. Shame is ugly and hard to acknowledge because it takes great self-awareness, courage, and vulnerability; unacknowledged shame is the most corrosive and destructive force of all. It takes bravery, curiosity, and resilience to annihilate it. You've got enough of all those traits now.

Remember that everything that happens in life and every single person who comes into your tiny corner of the world is here to teach you something. You're here to learn and grow and evolve. That process is going to be joyous *and* uncomfortable. Challenge yourself to stretch into uncomfortable territories.

At this point in my journey, I no longer experience regret. One could argue that everybody has regrets; we all wish we could have do-overs in life. But I return to knowing that, even when things don't happen the way I hope, it doesn't diminish my life in any way. It simply means that I've been asked to embark on a new and unexpected adventure. It also means that I had an expectation, which is a sign I'm not in the present moment and that I'll likely learn from that expectation by getting more comfortable with disappointment. After all, change lives in uncomfortable places.

That's life. The richness of falling down, of struggling, is not something I would ever want to avoid. We all go through experiences to activate the reservoir of resilience at our core. That way, when we finally connect with our Original Blueprint®, we're ready to embody it fully. Most of what happens in life is by design. Embrace it all.

I appreciate my life to a degree that I didn't know was possible. Every moment is sacred. I savor every breath. I savor my aliveness. I appreciate what I have and feel content with my life. I say my prayers of appreciation at night and find things to be thankful for comes much more easily for me now. *Life comes* to *me. Nature comes* to *me. Love comes* to *me.* The connection I've cultivated with my higher source is so strong now that we're in constant communication. And the most joyful feeling a human being can experience is that unconditional love.

I stay in my body. I breathe. I embrace the lessons that show up with each moment, each person, each interaction. My experiences all serve a greater purpose. Every moment is delicious and without judgment. There's nothing that happens to me or around me that isn't part of my growth and my journey.

Now that I understand how to maintain this connection to my Original Blueprint®, I relish this peaceful, fearless, courageous, spacious, joyful, loving presence. It's a hard thing to tangibly describe. But what is tangible is how I show up differently in every aspect of my life. My health is far better than it's ever been. Doing the rituals and exercises described in this book has enabled me to repair a lot of my health issues, along with many, many healers who've helped me along the way. I've healed my lingering emotional traumas. I feel physically, mentally, and spiritually vibrant. I know that within me is the capacity and resilience to get through anything.

If I sound like I've figured it all out, let me be clear: I am in no way perfect. I reserve the right to be imperfect! Perfection is boring, not to mention unattainable. Life is weird, wacky and one big surprise after another. I'd rather swim in life's murky mess and delight in it.

However you decide to move through your life, I hope that you heal and release fear, so that you can be in the richness of your own beautiful self—as present as possible in every moment. Crisis is a gift because times of crisis is when you begin to put things into perspective. Enduring at least one major crisis brings you face-to-face with the deeper facets of your character—the strength, determination, and flexibility—that you can then use to navigate anything. And you learn who will be by your side.

Being knocked about by the ebbs and flows of life is the equivalent to checking social media constantly to see how many people have "liked" us. When we get lots of "likes" and positive feedback, we're elated. We feel popular and admired. But when no one responds to our posts or, even worse, the responses are negative, we drop into depression. Don't let the winds of the moment pull you in either direction—rise above it.

If you choose to let external forces bandy you about, you'll find yourself at the mercy of the world, the fluctuations of life constantly knocking you off balance. The resolve with which you face life's ups and downs determines whether you'll be able to overcome hardships—like a powerful, majestic redwood. Lacking resolve, you'll eventually become gnarled and brittle, a tree whose roots are not firmly planted. When the rains come, the tree will topple.

But that all goes away when you realize that bravely meeting challenges without fear allows you to stay in the constant steadiness of your interior self. There's no need to respond to other people's judgments of you—or even your inner critic's judgment of you. That's all just gibberish—a never-ending stream of nonsense. Your Original Blueprint® is beyond such concerns. It's ripe with curiosity, joy, play and, most of all, love. It's free of both fear and judgment. It's a precious and present gem of ourselves that doesn't attach to an identity or move in whatever direction the wind blows.

Your Original Blueprint® doesn't resist the impermanence of life. For human beings, the primal root of all our fear is the fear of falling into an abyss, no longer relevant and forgotten after we die. But death is part of life; it's a gift to have an ending to things because it means that there's some new chapter coming. And we are clearing the way for an emergence of newness—here on earth and wherever our *energy* bodies go from here. How cool is that—we free our physical bodies and our souls return to the universe!

If you can release your fear of death by accepting it and return to the present moment, life becomes an infinite source of exponential joy. And any false notion of falling into nothingness is simply a paper tiger. Death is simply a shedding of the physical body. The essence of you that transcends this physical plane is your Original Blueprint®. It's who you were before you came into this world and the aspect of your soul you have now re-awakened. It will be central to who you truly are when you leave this planet.

So, stop worrying about the future. You can't predict what it will look like or when things will end. Whenever the end comes, let it be a beginning of something new. Until then, live your life to the fullest and live your legacy today. You want to leave a legacy for those who come after you to show them what it's like to live fearlessly and be in your full Original Blueprint®. You want to leave the world better than you found it.

Life is full of extraordinary moments that show you how thin the veil is between here and the other world (or worlds—who knows). Some people seek those moments of aliveness and wonderment, such as a daredevil who skydives from a plane or bungee jumps off a tall bridge. Sometimes those moments come unexpectedly, through near-death experiences that result from accidents or illness. And sometimes they come through traumatic experiences that leave us shaken and reassessing what's really important in life.

Regardless of how life ends up shaking you, those kinds of events can't help but leave you transformed. You don't have to have a radical experience to get there. Connecting with your Original Blueprint® will give you that sense of vitality in every moment. Every day becomes a new opportunity to face the veil fearlessly, with joy and gratitude in your heart and soul. Your Original Blueprint® is a beautiful reminder to be here fully, anchored in the wondrous beauty of the yummy, present moment.

Stay true to you.

REMEMBER

Go back to the first pages of this book where you set an intention for yourself. Now that you have concluded the book, see if what you imagined is different than what you have now, in any way. You can write about it in your journal or in the Companion Workbook.

APPENDICES

GLOSSARY OF TERMS

Activation: Also called arousal or hyperactivity, activation is the stimulation of the cerebral cortex into a state of general wakefulness, or attention.

Autonomic Nervous System: Regulates the involuntary responses of our bodies, including heart rate, digestion, and sexual arousal. It is responsible for sympathetic and parasympathetic responses, including fight, flight, and freeze.

Dysregulation: Emotional responses that are not well modulated. Also known as "reactivity."

Original Blueprint®: The purest form of the human expression of the soul.

Paper Tiger: Something or someone who appears threatening but is ineffectual. The illusion of danger.

Parasympathetic: The part of the nervous system that slows heart rate and increases intestinal activity. It is the "rest-and-digest" part of the autonomic nervous system.

Presence: The ability to notice a sensation of any kind in your body.

Reactivity: Acting in response to others or external stimuli. "Defensiveness" is often a synonym.

Sympathetic: The part of the nervous system that increases heart rate, blood pressure and pupil size. It's the get-up-and-go part of your nervous system and supports any action-oriented behavior.

Vagus Nerve: Complicated but simply put, it is the largest bundle of nerves in the body. It carries signals to and from most of your major, vital organs back to the brain.

Vagal Tone: Increasing vagal tone engages the parasympathetic nervous system, which allows your body to relax faster after stress.

Interoception: The perception of sensations from inside the body that includes the perception of physical sensations related to internal organ function such as heartbeat, respiration, satiety, and the autonomic nervous system activity related to emotions.

Microaggressions: Indirect, subtle, or unintentional discrimination against members of a marginalized group. For example, pulling one's purse closer in, eyes looking away, or avoiding a person of another race.

Proprioception: The body's ability to perceive its own position in space. For example, proprioception enables a person to close her eyes and touch her nose with an index finger, know whether feet are on soft grass or hard cement without looking (even while wearing shoes) or notice the support of a chair behind and underneath the body.

Regulation: the ability to manage our energy states, emotions, thoughts, and behaviors in ways that are acceptable and produce positive results such as well-being, loving relationships, and learning.

Somatic (or Soma): From the Greek language, meaning "Body."

Window of Resilience: The optimal range of capacity in our nervous systems to be able to navigate thoughts and emotions without overwhelm.

GLOSSARY OF SOMATIC DIMENSIONS
Add your own, plus any colors and images you experience!

Achy	Energized	Knotted
Airy	Expansive	Light
Alive	Faint	Limp
Aromatic	Fluid	Loose
Bloated	Flushed	Lukewarm
Blob	Fluttery	Nauseous
Blocked	Frantic	Neutral
Braced	Freezy	Numb
Breathless	Frigid	Octagonal
Brittle	Frosty	Oblong
Bubbly	Frozen	Open
Burning	Full	Paralyzed
Buzzing	Fuzzy	Pleasant
Calming	Geometric	Pounding
Chilling	Glowing	Pressure
Clammy	Goose Bumpy	Prickly
Closed	Gravitated	Puffy
Cloudy	Grounding	Pulled
Cold	Gurgling	Pulsing
Congested	Hard	Pungent
Constricted	Hazy	Quaking
Contracted	Heart-shaped	Quiet
Cool	Heavy	Quivering
Cozy	Held	Radiating
Cramped	Hot	Ragged
Cube	Icy	Raw
Dense	Intense	Rolling
Dizzy	Itchy	Round
Dully	Jagged	Safe
Elastic	Jittery	Salty
Electric	Jumbly	Savory
Empty	Jumpy	Shaky

Sharp
Shimmering
Shivery
Shudder
Silky
Smoky
Smooth
Soft
Soothing
Spacious
Spaciousness
Spasming
Spherical
Spicy
Square
Sticky
Still
Stretchy
Stringy
Strong
Suffocating

Sweaty
Sweet
Tender
Tense
Tepid
Thick
Throbbing
Tickly
Tight
Tingling
Trembling
Triangular
Twitchy
Unpleasant
Vibrating
Warm
Weak
Weighted
Wide-open
Wobbly
Wonderment

...or add your own!

_____

_____

_____

_____

Includes words from the five senses, sensations, emotions, shapes, temperatures, meaning.

GLOSSARY OF EMOTIONS

Abandoned
Able
Absorbed
Abused
Accepting
Accomplished
Adamant
Admirable
Admired
Affable
Affectionate
Afraid
Aggravated
Aggressive
Agony
Agreeable
Alarmed
Alert
Alienated
Aliveness
Alone
Amazed
Ambivalent
Amused
Angry
Annoyed
Anxious
Apprehensive
Ashamed
Astonished
Awed
Awkward

Baffled
Bashful
Bereaved
Bewildered
Bitter
Blissful
Blue
Bold
Bothered
Brave
Buoyant

Calm
Cantankerous
Capable
Carefree
Careful
Caring
Cautious
Chagrined
Charitable
Cheerful
Cold
Complacent
Composed
Compulsive
Concerned
Confident
Considerate
Contemptuous
Content
Contrite

Cooperative
Cranky
Crestfallen
Cross
Crushed
Curious

Daring
Defiant
Dejected
Delighted
Depressed
Detached
Determined
Devious
Disappointed
Discouraged
Disdainful
Disenchanted
Disengaged
Disgusted
Disillusioned
Disinterested
Dismayed
Dismissive
Distant
Doleful

Eager
Ecstatic
Edgy
Elated

Embarrassed
Emboldened
Enraged
Enthusiastic
Envious
Euphoric
Excited
Exhausted
Extravagant
Exuberant

Fair
Fatigued
Fearful
Flustered
Foolish
Forgiving
Frightened
Frustrated
Fulfilled
Funny
Furious

Generous
Glad
Gleeful
Gloomy
Glum
Gracious
Grateful
Greedy
Grief-stricken
Grouchy
Grumpy
Guarded
Guilty

Happy
Heartbroken
Helpless
Hesitant
Hopeless
Horrified
Humbled
Humiliated
Hurt
Hyperactive
Hypoactive
Hysterical

Ignorant
Ignored
Impatient
Impertinent
Inadequate
Indifferent
Inquisitive
Insecure
Inspired
Inspiring
Interested
Irked
Irrational
Irritable
Irritated
Isolated
Jaded
Jealous
Jittery
Jocular
Joyful
Joyous
Judged

Judgmental

Keen
Kind

Lackluster
Lazy
Leery
Lethargic
Listless
Lonely
Loving

Mad
Malevolent
Manic
Manipulated
Manipulative
Marvelous
Mean
Meek
Melancholy
Melodramatic
Mischievous
Miserable
Misunderstood
Moody
Mopey
Morose
Moved

Naïve
Nasty
Naughty

Needed

Needy

Neglected

Neglectful

Nervous

Nice

Nonchalant

Nonplussed

Numb

Obedient

Obligated

Obsessed

Obsessive

Obstinate

Offended

Open

Open-minded

Optimistic

Outraged

Overjoyed

Overloaded

Overpowered

Overstimulated

Overwhelmed

Panicked

Panicky

Passive

Peaceful

Peeved

Pensive

Perturbed

Petrified

Petty

Petulant

Placid

Playful

Pleased

Powerful

Powerless

Pressured

Prickly

Prideful

Preoccupied

Proud

Puzzled

Quiet

Quirky

Quivery

Quelled

Rageful

Rational

Rattled

Reasonable

Reasoned

Reassured

Rebellious

Refreshed

Rejuvenated

Relaxed

Relieved

Reluctant

Remorseful

Repulsed

Resentful

Reserved

Restless

Sad

Safe

Sanguine

Sarcastic

Satisfied

Scared

Scornful

Secure

Sensitive

Serene

Serious

Shy

Silly

Sincere

Skeptical

Smug

Sociable

Sorrowful

Spiteful

Startled

Stressed

Stubborn

Surprised

Sympathetic

Tearful

Teary

Temperamental

Tender

Terrified

Thankful

Thoughtful

Threatened

Tickled

Timid

Tired

Tiresome

Tolerable
Tolerant
Torn
Touched
Tranquil
Trepidatious
Troubled
Trusted
Trusting
Trustworthy

Unafraid
Unappreciated
Uncertain
Uncomfortable
Undecided
Uneasy
Unhappy
Unimpressed
Unnerved
Unruffled
Unruly
Unsteady
Unsure
Unwavering
Uplifted
Uptight
Useful
Useless

Vacant
Vain
Valuable
Valued
Vexed
Vibrant

Victimized
Victorious
Violent
Vital
Vivacious
Volatile
Vulnerable

Warm
Wary
Wasted
Weak
Weary
Weepy
Whimsical
Whiny
Willful
Willing
Wishful
Wistful
Withdrawn
Witty
Worn
Worried
Worthless
Wronged

Yearning
Yielding
Youthful
Zany
Zealous

SUGGESTED READINGS

Boyle, G. (2010). *Tattoos on the Heart: The power of boundless compassion.* Free Press.

Fisher, J. (2017). *Healing the Fragmented Selves of Trauma Survivors: Overcoming internal self-alienation.* Routledge.

Hanson, R., Hanson, F. (2018). *Resilient: How to grow an unshakable core of calm, strength, and happiness.* Harmony Books.

Kain, K., Terrell, S. (2018). *Nurturing Resilience: Helping clients move forward from developmental trauma.* North Atlantic Books.

Levine, A., Heller, R. (2010). *Attached: The new science of adult attachment and how it can help you find—and keep—love.* Penguin Group

Levine, P., Kline, M. (2008). *Trauma-Proofing Your Kids: A parent's guide for instilling confidence, joy, and resilience.* North Atlantic Books

Levine, P. (1997). *Waking the Tiger: Healing Trauma.* North Atlantic Books.

Lopez, I. (2014). *Dog Whistle Politics: How coded racial appeals have reinvented racism and wrecked the middle class.* Oxford University Press

Maté, Gabor. (2003). *When the Body Says No: Exploring the stress-disease connection.* John Wiley & Sons, Inc.

Menakem, R. (2017). *My Grandmother's Hands: Racialized trauma and the pathway to mending our hearts and bodies.* Central Recovery Press

Ogden, P., Minton, K., Pain, C. (2006). *Trauma and the Body: A sensorimotor approach to psychotherapy.* W.W. Norton & Company

Pinker, S. (2014). *The Village Effect: How face-to-face contact can make us healthier and happier.* Vintage Canada.

Schwartz, R. (2008). *You are the One You've Been Waiting For: Bringing courageous love to intimate relationships.* Trailheads Publications

Siegel, M.D., D., Hartzell, M.Ed., M. (2003)
Parenting from the Inside Out: How a deeper self-understanding can help you raise children who thrive. Penguin Random House

Strozzi-Heckler, R. (1984). *The Anatomy of Change: A way to move through life's transitions.* North Atlantic Books.

Van der Hart, O., Nijenhuis, E., Steele, K. (2006) *The Haunted self: Structural dissociation and the treatment of chronic traumatization.* W.W. Norton & Company, Inc.

Van Der Kolk, M.D., B. (2014). *The Body Keeps the Score: Brain, mind, and body in the healing of trauma.* Viking